In the Age of the Internet that ushered in this century, product was still king, and the Product Manager was the role around which everything else revolved. Today we are in the Age of the Customer, where the customer is king, and the role around which everything else must revolve is the Customer Success Manager. This is a new role, and that makes The Customer Success Professional's Handbook *a timely and welcome contribution across the globe. It is comprehensive, accurate, and incredibly well informed, making it a "must-read" for anyone performing, managing, or entering the profession.*

—Geoffrey A. Moore,
Author, *Crossing the Chasm* and *Zone to Win*

Business Success = Customer Success. When companies realize this truth, they'll want this handbook!
—Therese Tucker, CEO and Founder, BlackLine

Gainsight is the clear thought leader in Customer Success. This Professional's Handbook *teaches you how to scale Customer Success, drive up NPS and revenue retention, and get out ahead of the competition. Customer Success should be a science and not just an art. The* Handbook *helps you realize that.*
—Jason M. Lemkin, SaaStr CEO and Founder

Everyone agrees that Customer Success is a worthy and profitable goal for every company. It's the damn execution thing that gets in the way. And at the heart of execution lies the CSM. The Customer Success Professional's Handbook *is the most comprehensive book that's ever been written on the critical steps for successfully implementing CS at scale. For CSMs in particular, the* Handbook *not only communicates what needs to be done but how and why. Ashvin and Ruben have brought together key insights from Gainsight's vast experience along with some of the industry's top CS executives to create a book that should be in the minds and on the desk of every CS professional.*
—J.B. Wood, President and CEO, TSIA

Imagine Ramsay, Keller, Ducasse, Bourdain, Blumenthal all collaborating on the ultimate guide to becoming a chef. That's what the vanguard of the modern Customer

Success movement has done here to help budding Customer Success professionals earn their chef's hat. This is a straight-up cookbook for one of the most important recipes in business growth today – the Customer Success organization.

—Jay Simons, President, Atlassian

The Customer Success Professional's Handbook *is a must-read for CSM practitioners at all levels. Putting the customer at the center should be a key component of a company's overall strategy. Businesses are recognizing this and the CSM role is growing in influence across industries as a result. This one-of-a-kind guide from leading experts in the field provides practitioners with actionable insights and advice to help them drive growth for their companies and succeed in their careers. A must-read for customer-facing professionals!*

—Yamini Rangan, Chief Customer Officer, Dropbox

Customer Success is a critical component of any subscription business. It's not just about the technology but how to ensure users and companies gain continuous business value from your product. Many organizations are struggling to define how best to do this. Ashvin and Ruben do an incredible job of taking you step-by-step to define and build a successful Customer Success organization. It is a must-read for any founder, CEO, executive, and Customer Success professional looking to understand the critical value Customer Success plays in the subscription economy.

—Christina Kosmowski, VP,
Global Head of Customer Success, Slack

Ashvin and Ruben have designed required reading for anyone in a Customer Success role – or really, anyone who works with customers. Companies cemented in the past are still searching for ways to automate the humanity out of customer relationships. The companies that will win the next era of business know that the technology-empowered human will always be at the center of their relationships. That human is a CSM, and this is the only guide with everything they need to create customers for life.

—Nick Mehta, CEO, Gainsight,
Co-Author, *Customer Success*

The Customer Success Professional's Handbook *is a critical resource for those in the Customer Success space or trying to better understand it. Ashvin and Ruben have lived this world in the trenches and understand the necessity and the challenges of the Customer Success role. Because the CS org and the CSM function will be critical to your long-term success as a business, this book is a must-read for those on the ground as well as those in leadership.*

**—Dan Steinman, GM of EMEA, Gainsight,
Co-Author, *Customer Success***

With the explosion of Customer Success as a function and one of the most exciting and rewarding careers for the upcoming decade, there has been a need for the definitive how-to guide for Customer Success professionals. The Customer Success Professional's Handbook *fills this need with expert insights from industry professionals and the amazing thought leadership from Ruben and Ashvin, two known experts in the space. This is a must-read for not only CS professionals but anyone looking to build a customer-centric organization, the key to thriving in a world where customers have a plethora of choices and are in the driver's seat of deciding who to build longstanding partnerships with.*

—Wendi C. Sturgis, CEO, Yext Europe

In the Digital Age where the customer is at the center of everything, The Customer Success Professional's Handbook *isn't just for customer-facing teams. Everyone – from Product teams and Developers to Marketing organizations and Sales – will gain insights into the mind of the customer and will come away being able to make decisions that drive better outcomes for their customers.*

—Aaron Levie, CEO and Co-Founder, Box

For many years, people have tried to capture the essence of Customer Success and the role of the CS professional. Ruben and Ashvin's The Customer Success Professional's Handbook *was designed to inform, educate, and give the CS professional guidance on the day-to-day procedures of the CSM, CS professional, and executive. In my many years in the Customer Success industry, this is the first book that encompasses all of the valuable information you will need to succeed in one place.*

—Rachel Orston, Chief Customer Officer, BetterCloud

The Customer Success Professional's Handbook is a must-read for every customer-facing professional in a SaaS business. Irrespective of your role or the stage of your business, this book needs to be within arm's reach as you formulate and operationalize your Customer Success disciplines. As the authors passionately point out, Customer Success is both a critical mindset and a team sport, and they have packed this guide with great examples and models that you can implement across your organization. As a leader who has focused my entire career on Customer Success, I am re-inspired to spring into action with new ideas.

—Chris Comparato, CEO of Toast, Inc.

As the global economy fundamentally shifts toward becoming a subscription economy, the role of the Customer Success leader is critical to protect and grow your customer base and, in turn, establish category and market leadership. Whether you are a CEO looking to transform your business to be more customer-centric, a Chief Customer Officer, or an aspiring Customer Service Leader, this is a must-read!

—Ajay Agarwal, Partner at Bain Capital Ventures

THE
CUSTOMER
SUCCESS
PROFESSIONAL'S
HANDBOOK

THE CUSTOMER SUCCESS

PROFESSIONAL'S HANDBOOK

How to Thrive in One of the World's Fastest Growing
Careers—While Driving Growth For Your Company

ASHVIN VAIDYANATHAN | RUBEN RABAGO

WILEY

Published by John Wiley & Sons, Inc., Hoboken, New Jersey.
Published simultaneously in Canada.

For general information on our other products and services or for technical support, please contact our Customer Care Department within the United States at (800) 762–2974, outside the United States at (317) 572–3993 or fax (317) 572–4002.

Wiley publishes in a variety of print and electronic formats and by print-on-demand. Some material included with standard print versions of this book may not be included in e-books or in print-on-demand. If this book refers to media such as a CD or DVD that is not included in the version you purchased, you may download this material at http://booksupport.wiley.com. For more information about Wiley products, visit www.wiley.com.

Library of Congress Cataloging-in-Publication Data is Available:

ISBN 9781119624615 (Hardcover)
ISBN 9781119624622 (ePDF)
ISBN 9781119624639 (ePub)

Developmental Editor: Martta Eicher-Rabago
Cover Design & Image: © Hayley Cromwell
Cover Concept: Anthony Kennada

Printed in the United States of America

SKY10031662_112921

DEDICATED TO
The Gainsight Product & Engineering Teams
and to our family and friends

Contents

Contributors

Alan Armstrong, CEO, Eigenworks

Carine Roman, Global Head of Customer Success at LinkedIn Talent Solutions

Chad Horenfeldt, VP of Client Success, Updater

Chrisy Woll, VP of Customer Success, CampusLogic

David Kocher, VP of Customer Success, GE Digital

Easton Taylor, Director of Customer Success, Gainsight

Eduarda Camacho, Executive VP, Customer Operations at PTC

Elaine Cleary, Principal CSM, Director of Education Services, Gainsight

Erin Siemens, SVP Client Success, ADP

John Sabino, Chief Customer Officer, Splunk

Jon Herstein, Chief Customer Officer, Box

Mary Poppen, Chief Customer Officer, Glint

Nadav Shem-Tov, Director of Teammate Success-CS, Gainsight

Patrick Eichen, VP Client Success, Cornerstone OnDemand

Stephanie Berner, Global Head of Customer Success at LinkedIn Sales Solutions

Travis Kaufman, VP of Product Growth, Gainsight

Foreword

In 1999, I joined a start-up in San Francisco that had the bizarre idea that it could sell business software in the same way Amazon sold books: via the cloud. Needless to say, my friends thought I was crazy. Crazy as it seemed, I jumped into the new venture. I was employee number 13 at Salesforce, and the second sales hire for the company.

I quickly learned that doing business in the cloud required an entirely different mindset. The nature of the subscription model that Salesforce created made it easy for customers to leave if they felt they weren't getting value from their investment in our Customer Relationship Management technology. There were no more long-term, lock-in contracts that defined the on-premise solutions dominating the software industry at the time. We knew if our renewal rates trended in the wrong direction, Salesforce would not be able to survive for long.

In those early days, we began to see renewal rates going in the wrong direction, and we knew that we needed to make a fundamental change in how we engaged with customers. We quickly understood that our success was tightly coupled with the success of our customers. We had to find a better way to keep them happy.

That crisis actually helped us to focus on solving for the customer, and in turn, we innovated a new kind of job. Salesforce created a role singularly focused on making sure customers were getting the most value out of using our product.

That role was the Customer Success Manager (CSM).

From there, we created a team of CSMs. Their entire job was to address customer concerns, help them better use our technology, and collect key feedback that we could use to improve our products. These people had domain expertise, problem-solving, and communication skills. They became trusted advisors for our customers.

Today, our cadre of CSMs is an integral part of the Customer Success Group, which has more than 7000 people dedicated to driving success for the company's 150 000-plus customers. So, when Ashvin and Ruben first told me they were writing a new book on customer success, I was hoping they would focus on the essential role CSMs play in driving growth, increasing retention, and reducing churn. Both of them are consummate professionals who know first-hand what it takes to achieve customer success in this era of digital transformation.

I was thrilled to see that they went beyond my expectations. They have delivered the definitive working handbook for Customer Success Managers everywhere. *The Customer Success Professional's Handbook* explains how to break into this fast-growing profession and describes the core skills needed to become a truly great CSM. It also explores how CSMs can operationalize success, and how companies can attract and retain top CSM talent.

It's a comprehensive overview, and I believe it will appeal to every CSM at every stage in their career; from entry-level to Chief Customer Officer.

Brian Millham
President
Global Customer Success, Salesforce

THE
CUSTOMER
SUCCESS
PROFESSIONAL'S
HANDBOOK

What Is Customer Success and Why Is It a Great Career?

1 | Customer Success Management: The Birth of a New Profession

- The role of the Customer Success Manager (CSM) has seen a 736% increase since 2015[1] and is one of the most promising professions according to LinkedIn.[2]
- Companies that consider Customer Success (CS) as a strategic priority saw higher improvement in metrics, with roughly twice the number of companies reporting a double-digit improvement in renewal rates according to Deloitte.[3]
- Customer Success Manager has the highest Career Advancement score possible, according to proprietary LinkedIn data.[4]
- 60% of Customer Success professionals have received a base-salary increase in the last 12 months while in their current roles.[5]

THIS is why you have chosen the Customer Success profession. Even if it chose you, be emboldened because Customer Success Management is one of the hottest and most promising modern jobs of the twenty-first century. Companies, especially those that are subscription-based, are finding they cannot survive without it. Those who have embraced Customer Success as a practice are growing faster than their competition. To no surprise, the role of a Customer Success Manager is at the center of this digital transformation.

From an executive's perspective, having an effective Customer Success Management team maximizes a company's value because it generates revenue from existing accounts more efficiently than acquiring new logos.[6] The growth is due largely to Customer Success Managers creating essential relationships with existing customers and driving value for them. Businesses are listening because of the results. They are converting to the way of Customer Success. What does that mean for you as a current or future CS professional? Endless opportunities!

Because of the current business landscape, the customer's requirements have evolved. Customers expect outcomes, not just a completed transaction. Businesses have realized they must deliver value in a way that fulfills their product's promise and meets clients' expectations. Enter Customer Success! The CS function is the bridge between customer expectations, the experience they receive, and ultimately their retention. As a result, Customer Success is now one of the most significant contributors to company growth. In 2016, McKinsey & Company published a report that was titled "Grow Fast or Die Slow: Focusing on Customer Success to Drive Growth." They concluded, "Ultimately, the focus on customer success not only accelerates revenue growth but also creates a more efficient and effective go-to-market organization."[7]

Despite the excitement surrounding this burgeoning industry, many are just discovering this fresh new job role and function. You could be an executive looking to advance your business, or an existing Customer Success Manager looking to refine your craft. Some are aspiring to jump into a relatively easy-to-enter profession. No matter what your starting point is, be excited! This comparatively new profession is not just a fad. Companies across a variety of industries have adopted the approach. The Customer Success professional is not a retitling of existing positions either. Customer Success is a new mindset, and the role of Customer Success Manager is its ambassador.

CS has become a critical contributing factor to a company's growth engine, and people know it. In his blog, Tomasz Tunguz, Venture Capitalist at Redpoint and SaaS performance expert, summarized his verdict at a panel discussion on the topic. He stated, "Customer success is transforming SaaS companies by increasing revenue growth, decreasing capital needs, building better products and consequently retaining more customers."[8] The spawning of the Customer Success movement may have begun with SaaS and the subscription model, but it is starting to permeate nearly every industry and business segment.[9]

A great example of a company that has taken full advantage of this functional and digital transformation focus on building *their customers'* businesses is Adobe. They transitioned from a typical and traditional software delivery approach to a subscription-based licensing model. The results were spectacular. Thomas Lee of the *San Francisco Chronicle* captured Adobe's resurgence in a 2017 article stating, "once dismissed as a 'relic of the bygone era of boxed desktop software,' Adobe has transformed itself into a cloud powerhouse serving other big businesses in just three years."[10]

The bold move allowed Adobe to scale faster and granted greater flexibility to their business and their customers, resulting in a significant usage increase of their platform products (Figure 1.1). Of course, they have an amazing Customer Success team that helped to fuel this growth! On 27 March 2019, Adobe's CEO, Shantanu Narayen, noted during his keynote address at the Adobe Summit convention that "The subscription model put the customer experience front and centre. And we became a company that embraced the always-on reality of the digital business, delivering a

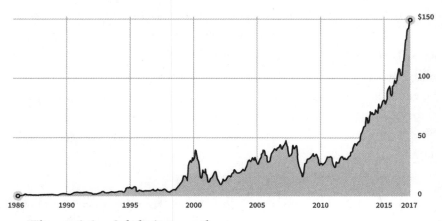

Figure 1.1   Adobe's growth.

continuous stream of innovation to our customers and focusing on building our customer's business and trust every single day."[11]

John Sabino, Chief Customer Officer at Splunk, also subscribes to the correlation between Customer Success and business success. A titan in the CS industry, John has an impressive resumé, including executive leadership roles at GE Digital and NBC Universal. But what truly compelled us to ask John to share his thoughts on the topic, is his perpetual determination to promote cross-functional excellence and his focus on the customer's success:

> The most successful companies will be the ones who place importance on creating a company culture focused on delivering scalable value to customers across all operations and processes. CEOs and their commercial leaders must be "obsessed with customer success" and appropriately plan and allocate resources to this functional discipline in order to retain their current customer base and grow revenue in an often-uncertain macro-economic environment.
>
> By its nature, Customer Success forces executive teams to see products and services from your customers' perspective. In doing so, Customer Success helps infuse companies with innovations from the perspective of your customers. Ultimately, without this "customer-in" view, a company can and will waste resources on capabilities that do not produce customer value, and they risk making their company irrelevant in the marketplace of the future.

Customer Success is a real function that is creating actual results, and the future is only growing brighter with incredible promise. Curiosity about the remarkable growth is even reflected in the trend of Google Searches (Figure 1.2) on the phrase "customer success manager."[12]

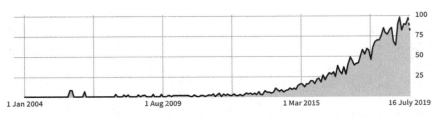

Figure 1.2   Google Trends on "Customer Success Manager."

The CSM role, more often than not, chooses the employee, not the other way around. There is a 100% certainty that no one grew up dreaming they wanted to be a CSM. It is also 100% certain you did not come out of college wanting to be a CSM either. Up until 2017, there wasn't even a university-level course covering the topic. Dr. Vijay Mehrotra of the University of San Francisco started a career accelerator program for MBA students with an emphasis on Customer Success and Business Analytics. About a year later, Dr. Bryan Hochstein launched a full semester graduate-level course exclusively on the topic of Customer Success Manager at the University of Alabama in the fall of 2018. Some professors have started to introduce CS concepts into their curriculum, like Dr. Deva Rangarajan, Associate Professor of Marketing at Ball State University. You should also see Customer Success begin to make appearances in academic texts starting in 2020. It is inevitable that more universities and colleges will jump on this rocket ship to better prepare their students for this booming career.

No matter your journey thus far, Customer Success has come your way. If you are the executive that is responsible for leading your company's CS initiatives, you are likely still trying to figure out how best to structure your team to ensure all the accounts receive appropriate coverage and attention. What is the right CSM-to-customer ratio? How do I keep great CSMs from leaving? What is the best practice for promoting and career advancement for CSMs? What is the best variable compensation model?

If you are a Customer Success Manager that came into this role, by choice or by chance, consider yourself fortunate. If you can elevate the skills and best practices of what it takes to be a great CSM, you will likely have a long and rewarding career in this field. Even more, there is tremendous transferability of your skills and experience to many other business disciplines. Take, for instance, the two authors of this book. Both of us started as CSMs at Gainsight®. Like us, many of our peers accelerated into Product Management, Marketing, Sales, Sales Consultants and Engineering, Teammate Success or Human Resources, Business Development, Operations, Leadership, and more. The skills acquired and refined as a CSM literally can serve as a catalyst to every role imaginable. And the opportunities keep growing. As of June 2019, a search on LinkedIn for all open Customer Success – related job postings worldwide that were no more than one-month-old resulted in 153 654 listings, 30% of which were outside of the United States.[13]

According to Nick Mehta, CEO of the category-creating customer success company, Gainsight, "The rapid advancement of SaaS and cloud technology has opened up doors that we couldn't have fathomed even five years ago, like the customer success manager role, which has quickly become one of the most sought after positions."[14] Nick is right! Industry data and the most successful companies in the world agree.

On 3 July 2017, Microsoft announced a significant structural change that introduced a new Customer Success organization. It was the final response to Microsoft's CEO, Satya Nadella's bold move to the cloud announced four years prior. John Jester, then Vice President of Worldwide Customer Success at Microsoft, told this story at the Pulse 2018 conference in front of over 5000 Customer Success professionals gathered in the Bay Area, California. Jester highlighted that a team formed from zero grew to over 1700 people in about a year. That was just the start. The remarkable underlying story is that these resources are not billable – they are a purposeful investment by Microsoft to ensure their customers are successful in attaining value from Microsoft's growing cloud offerings. Jester went on to quote Microsoft's CFO Amy Hood, who said, "Customer Success has become an obsession with Microsoft's sprawling cloud business . . . Because ultimately, in a consumption-based business, customer success is all that matters."[15]

Another example of a world–class company leaning into customer success is Cisco. According to the 8 March 2018 Doyle Report entitled "Customer Success Programs Contribute to the Rise in Recurring Revenue for Cisco Partners," Cisco's Senior Vice President of Customer Success, Scott Brown, convinced CEO Chuck Robbins and the executive leadership team to invest in Customer Success programs across the company. The report stated that Brown expected to "spend as much as $100 million on programs and tools, and hire 500 new people to ensure their success."[16] Shortly after that, Cisco made an even more impressive move towards Customer Success with the hiring of former president and head of the Global Customer Success group at Salesforce, Maria Martinez.[17]

The proof is there. The data is there. The examples are there. Do not wait for any more evidence to make CS a part of your company or organization or to jump into the profession. There is more than enough substantiation that this will be profitable for your business and yourself. If you are an experienced CSM looking to further your career, take every opportunity you can to advance your skillset. Consider Customer Success certification or related skills training. No matter where you are as a professional, you have hit this profession at the right time, and this book can be your guide as you take your next steps forward.

Now, let's explore the functional gaps that helped to define the role of Customer Success Manager. Understanding this brief history will help you better comprehend any remaining biases. It will also bring to light the impact that CSMs can have on customers and your company's growth.

The Age of the Customer

In 2004, there was an ever-increasing pressure building in Silicon Valley, as computing began to shift from distributed computing to "the cloud" and the concept of "Software as a Service" (SaaS). What quickly followed was the subscription business model era, which distributed the one-time large upfront payment across annual or monthly terms. Tech trends like cloud computing, SaaS, big data, social media, Google search, and mass migration to mobile devices made it easier to offer customers products and services without long-term contracts. The transition from a transactional economy (selling products) to a subscription economy (requiring repeat customers) created a seismic shift in power from companies to customers, and especially from software vendors to software buyers. The pivot to subscription-based solutions had a significant impact on the software industry, and it is still resonating today.

In Zuora's March 2019 annual analysis, "The Subscription Economy Index™," Chief Data Scientist, Carl Gold, reported that "subscription business sales have grown substantially faster than two key public benchmarks – S&P 500 Sales and U.S. retail sales. Overall, the SEI data reveals that subscription businesses grew revenues about five times faster than S&P 500

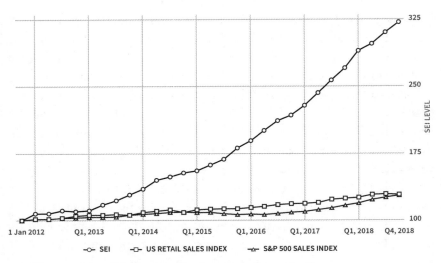

Figure 1.3   The subscription economy index.

company revenues (18.1% versus 3.6%) and U.S. retail sales (18.1% versus 3.8%) from January 1, 2012, to December 31, 2018." (Figure 1.3.)[18]

Born-in-the-cloud companies, such as Salesforce, have flourished with the new subscription model because of one key metric—Customer Lifetime Value or LTV for short—which essentially projects recurring revenue like it was an annuity. It is a lagging indicator that you want to maximize. Salesforce, from the outset, has been the most prolific company in the world to capitalize on this metric. Their trail to their current market cap of $121.71 billion (Figure 1.4) fundamentally gave birth to the Customer Success movement. It can unequivocally be stated that Salesforce's innovative approach to shifting the customer to the center of the vendor-buyer ecosystem and their resulting financial success was the catalyst for an entirely new profession: the Customer Success Manager. Salesforce's pivotal role in Customer Success is well summarized in the first chapter of *Customer Success: How Innovative Companies are Reducing Churn and Growing Recurring Revenue*.[19] Marc Benioff and the other founding Salesforce executives were initially delighted to discover they created a stream of nearly 20 000 customers in only four years since the company's launch. The primary driver was the low monthly subscription price per user as compared with the substantial upfront costs often required when

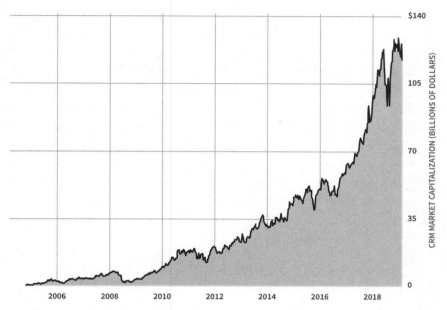

Figure 1.4   Salesforce market cap as of 21 June 2019. Illustration from Microtrends.[20]

companies purchased perpetual licenses for traditional enterprise software. Despite their success in attracting new customers, Salesforce was losing its customers at 8% per month. That is a 96% customer-churn annually. The low "consumer-like" pricing meant customers were not as committed or rather "held hostage" to a substantial software investment. In other words, it was far less painful for them to quit if they were not getting all the value from the service they had expected. It seemed like the new industry was bleeding, and executives were in a rush to avert the implosion brought on by a mass customer exodus. Acquiring customers faster than they were losing them was not a successful winning strategy.

The rules of business had changed. It was not enough for companies to land the big whale sale and then forget about that customer and move on. It was not enough that customers used your product or service. It was not enough that they logged into your platform. It did not even matter if they were using your product precisely as you designed it. You had to make your clients succeed while using your products or services in this new age – the age of the customer. Instead of a sale happening once, subscription businesses had to "sell" to the same customer consistently – or they would cancel their subscription.

Suddenly, the 800 number that you provided to your customers for friendly live technical support would not suffice. Customers expected to start seeing value from their subscription products immediately after the purchase. Customers also expected you to provide best practices along with strategic and tactical advice on using your solutions.

If you could not or would not pivot toward making your customers successful, be certain they were already talking with an eager and more nimble competitor. Making the switch was just a mouse-click away. There was no customer loyalty anymore. Everything transitioned to the benefit of the buyer, the consumer, the customer, the human decision-maker.

The Critical Missing Function

In the search to stop the process of customer departures, a positive came out of the negative: the creation of not only a new philosophy but a new role. That is when customer retention became the center of the SaaS world. Gone were the days when you could hold your customer hostage with the massive investments they made in your solutions. When software companies moved to the cloud, all a customer needed was a web browser and a computer to operate their new digital purchases.

For the companies selling the software, primarily via a subscription model, they soon realized a vacancy existed in their operational motions. Marketing was busy creating demand and qualified leads. Sales were busy working the pipeline and closing new business. Professional Services was busy implementing and getting customers started on their journey. All the while, Support was reacting to customer questions that were break-fix in nature, rarely proactive, and never strategic.

No one function was responsible for making sure that the customer was attaining their desired expectations. More importantly, no one was ultimately responsible for ensuring the customer would stay a customer and buy more stuff from you. They definitely would not become a raving fan of your company, freely advocating your greatness to their social media feeds, your prospects, and your industry.

This functional gap was the inception of the Customer Success role. It created a new business imperative: the customer's success was directly tied to company success. This new era of subscription-based pricing placed growing pressure on boards of directors, executives, and operational leaders to no longer be complacent about their customers after that initial sale. They no longer had a guarantee that the once multi-million-dollar paying customer with a five- to ten-year capital investment would remain indefinitely. Like Salesforce, the industry realized you could no longer acquire your way to success. Selling to new customers is really expensive. According to KBCM Technology Group's 2019 SaaS Survey Results, the cost to acquire one dollar of new customer Annual Recurring Revenue (ARR) is $1.34 while the cost of expansion revenue from an existing customer is only 50 cents (Figure 1.5).[21] In other words, investing in customer retention and expansion programs, such as Customer Success, is essentially a more efficient new-revenue spend.

The SaaS industry woke up to these straightforward realities. Well, some of them did. Many dismissed the signals to their detriment. When

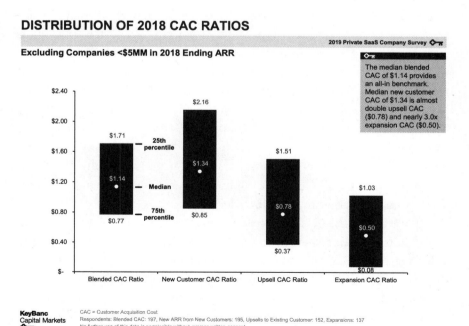

DISTRIBUTION OF 2018 CAC RATIOS

2019 Private SaaS Company Survey

Excluding Companies <$5MM in 2018 Ending ARR

The median blended CAC of $1.14 provides an all-in benchmark. Median new customer CAC of $1.34 is almost double upsell CAC ($0.78) and nearly 3.0x expansion CAC ($0.50).

KeyBanc Capital Markets

CAC = Customer Acquisition Cost
Respondents: Blended CAC: 197, New ARR from New Customers: 195, Upsells to Existing Customer: 152, Expansions: 137
No further use of this data is permissible without express written consent

Figure 1.5   Cost of revenue.

the Customer Success role first started to evolve, it was viewed by some as a fad and lacked clear responsibilities and disciplines. Perhaps it was a form of account management? Maybe it was a part of services and support? Still, more businesses were reaping the benefits of their Customer Success organizations and influence. Not only was CS keeping customers by fostering relationships and driving value for the customer, but they were also creating growing revenue through the established customer base – and doing it at a fraction of the cost of acquiring new logos. The market started to notice, and the role of Customer Success evolved. More evidence began to appear that Customer Success Manager efforts were working. Yes, there were still the skeptics that passed it off as a trend. However, highly respected institutions and publications were producing studies and articles stating that Customer Success was not only needed but was also succeeding.

In October 2015, *Harvard Business Review* published an article called "How smart, connected products are transforming companies." The authors, Michael E. Porter and James E. Heppelmann, proposed a third unit to the traditional software business organizational chart – the role of Customer Success Management. This unit sat below IT, R&D, Manufacturing, Marketing, Sales, Service, and Support. It was literally at the bottom of the totem pole. Yet, it was responsible for developing and creating relationships with customers that improved the customer experience, educated them to engage with the product, and created retention and renewals. Porter and Heppelmann believed that Customer Success management provided a needed function. They even asserted that the Customer Success unit was "crucial with smart, connected products, especially to ensure renewals in product-as-a-service models." They went on to state that "The customer success management unit does not necessarily replace sales or service units but assumes primary responsibility for customer relationships after the sale."[22]

It was 20 years since the birth of cloud computing. It was a decade since Customer Success emerged out of the SaaS industry to save it. People still were not seeing the value of Customer Success as a role or a team. To many, it was still too new to operate as an entity unto itself on the org-chart, despite the fact that it performed roles that Sales and Services teams would not and could not do. For one, CS was held to performance metrics that Sales did not want, such as monitoring product use, examining performance data, and tracking customer value. Even if they were asked to, Sales was incentivized and too busy hunting for new business. As for services, they also were not inclined to the day-to-day customer-facing duties of developing a relationship of advocacy and trust because they were in the "implementation-checklist" mindset and seeking out new transactional-based services to sell.

It is interesting to note that Porter and Heppelmann did propose a need for cross-organization integration. To them, it was essential. They also believed that creating alignment within a company was imperative for their customers. This alignment had to fit into the company's business plan and strategy. They thought that the functions should coordinate and manage critical handoffs in the product lifecycle. All of this was to "capture feedback from the field that [would] improve processes and products." However, the authors didn't completely conceive of who should lead that integration and who should benefit from it – was Customer Success truly conceived as the possible "glue" to hold the processes of integration together?

The authors' insights were great, but how could they foresee the writing on the wall? While their intentions were about making the customer successful, the means to that end weren't devised until a few years later.

The Birth of the Customer Success Manager

Meanwhile, Customer Success teams were changing the manner of customer engagements. It did not matter where the CS team was in an organization. They were having an amazing impact on companies. In the past, businesses relied heavily on customer surveys and call centers to collect insights about product use. They were somewhat trying to determine when a customer relationship was in an unstable state. Companies typically heard most from customers when something went wrong – and often not until it was too late. This methodology depended too much on lagging measurements. Slowly, companies saw the need for earlier intervention and early indicators of customer health. Perhaps even proactive investigation. The operational motions of Customer Success were maturing.

New software platforms and products were developed to help monitor the value customers were attaining from a product's use. The generated data could convey insights about a customer's experience. It revealed facts about product use and performance, customer preferences, and customer satisfaction. With this type of awareness and a relationship established, it prevented customers from defecting. Leveraging these leading customer health metrics also revealed where a customer could benefit from additional product capabilities or services. Everything was pointing towards customer retention, renewal, and growing revenue, mainly due to the direct intervention of a skilled Customer Success Manager.

The same year that Porter and Heppelmann's article was published, Gainsight's Pulse 2015 conference took place. This venue was becoming a site where experts in the field of SaaS and, now, Customer Success, could share their thoughts, insights, findings, and predictions. It was Jason Lemkin, then Managing Director of Storm Ventures and SaaS maven at SaaStr, who claimed: "Customer success is where 90% of the revenue is." Perhaps others were saying it too, but Lemkin shouted it. He spoke with knowledge and experience.

Lemkin grew a company called EchoSign from literally zero revenue to one hundred million dollars in Annual Recurring Revenue (ARR) in seven years. It was acquired by Adobe not long after. Lemkin attributed this to the fact that he heavily invested in customer success. In a *Forbes* magazine article called "Customer Success: the best-kept secret of hyper-growth startups," the author Alex McClafferty pronounced that "The term customer success may sound like a new Silicon Valley buzzword, but to SaaS pioneers such as Lemkin and companies such as Box and Atlassian, customer success can be the difference between failure and hyper-growth."[23]

It was a wake-up call. If start-ups had figured it out, were established companies going to follow? The SaaS industry was taking notice that Customer Success was not a fad anymore. CS grew beyond the prevention of high churn rates. There was more to it. Customer Success was becoming a business imperative. Companies were finding that with just a 5% increase in customer retention rates, a company could potentially yield profit increases anywhere from 25% to 95%.[24]

Moreover, there was a direct correlation between a company's performance and the level of maturity of Customer Success practices within that company. In 2017, Customer Success industry leader, Gainsight, reported (Figure 1.6 and1.7):[25]

REACTIVE	INSIGHTS & ACTIONS	OUTCOMES	TRANSFORM
Manage escalation on a case-by-case basis	Turn data into meaningful actions across your team	Proactively deliver customer outcomes at scale	Rally your entire company around the mission of Customer Success

Figure 1.6   Customer Success maturity.

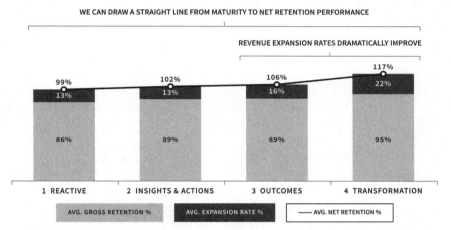

Figure 1.7   Net retention performance by Customer Success maturity.

As your organization matures, your business benefits from growth along four key drivers: improved retention, expansion, increased advocacy, and improved efficiency across your teams. Looking across different organizations, we identified four stages of Customer Success Maturity: Reactive, Insights & Actions, Outcomes, and Transformation.

This is critical. We've observed that as teams advance from stage to stage (based on <u>objective criteria</u>), it aligns with measurable increases in net retention. Between Reactive and Insights & Actions, there's a 3% increase in net retention rate (NRR). From Insights & Actions to Outcomes we see a 4% increase. And from Outcomes to Transformation there's a massive 11% jump.

The shift was and is real. The SaaS model would wither without Customer Success. The 2016 McKinsey & Company article titled "Grow fast or die slow: focusing on customer success to drive growth" was prophetic.[26] The proclamation was that SaaS could not survive without Customer Success. We agree. As does Carine Roman, Global Head of Customer Success for Talent Solutions at LinkedIn. When we asked her to comment on the CS movement and about the CS profession, she put it succinctly:

> Customer Success is a big deal. I believe the CS discipline is an essential competitive advantage that creates unique experiences and value for customers. Customer Success is not just a function. It needs to be a company state of mind and has to start at the top, at the C-level, where customer success obsession is intentional, not a "nice to have" and not the responsibility of a sole team.

What had not yet been said or defined were the skills and standards to become a great Customer Success Manager. Where would the explosion of growth take this profession? Let's find out.

Endnotes

1. Gainsight® (2019). The State of the Customer Success Profession 2019, May 2019. Retrieved from: https://www.gainsight.com/press/release/new-study-powered-by-linkedin-data-reveals-customer-success-growing-736-among-top-10-fastest-growing-professions/.
2. LinkedIn (2019). LinkedIn's Most Promising Jobs of 2019, 10 January 2019. Retrieved from: https://blog.linkedin.com/2019/january/10/linkedins-most-promising-jobs-of-2019.
3. Deloitte (2019). 2019 Enterprise Customer Success (CS) Study and Outlook: Fostering an Organization-wide CS Mindset. Retrieved from: https://www2.deloitte.com/us/en/pages/consulting/articles/state-of-customer-success-management.html?id=us:2el:3pr:cs:awa:cons:052019.
4. Roman, Carine (2018). Keynote presentation at Pulse 2018 Customer Success Conference "LinkedIn on the Future of the CSM Profession," May 2018. Retrieved from: https://gainsight.hubs.vidyard.com/watch/XdGimvQiN5vDhzeSCod4n5?.
5. Gainsight (2019). Customer Success Industry Benchmark Survey of nearly 700 Customer Success Professionals, September 2019.
6. JMSearch (2015). Customer Success: Unlocking Growth from Existing Accounts in SaaS Companies, citing 2015 Pacific Crest Survey of Private

SaaS Companies, Retrieved from: https://www.google.com/url? q=https://jmsearch.com/customer-success-unlocking-growth-from-existing-accounts-in-saas-companies-2/&sa=D& ust=1561090677440000&usg=AFQjCNEdoYBBNPFQNLKEE3-B1QWYLXYk-w.

7. Miller, M., Vonwiller, B., Weed, P., and McKinsey & Company (2016). Grow Fast or Die Slow: Focusing on Customer Success to Drive Growth. Retrieved from: https://www.mckinsey.com/industries/high-tech/our-insights/grow-fast-or-die-slow-focusing-on-customer-success-to-drive-growth.

8. Tungunz, T. (2014). The 4 Challenges Facing Customer Success Teams in SaaS Startups, 15 May 2014. Retrieved from: https://tomtunguz.com/four-challenges-facing-customer-success-teams/.

9. Atkins, C., Shobhit, G., Roche, P., and McKinsey & Company (2018). Introducing Customer Success 2.0: The New Growth Engine, January 2018. Retrieved from: https://www.mckinsey.com/~/media/McKinsey/Industries/High%20Tech/Our%20Insights/Introducing %20customer%20success%202%200%20The%20new%20growth %20engine/Introducing-customer-success-2–0-The-new-growth-engine.ashx.

10. Lee, T. (2017). Adobe's remarkable transformation, from Photoshop to cloud. *San Francisco Chronicle* (22 July 2017). Retrieved from: https://www.sfchronicle.com/business/article/Adobe-s-remarkable-transformation-from-11306625.php.

11. Birmingham, A. (2019). Adobe CEO, Shantanu Narayen, explains why the company had to transform. *Which-50* (27 March 2019). Retrieved from: https://which-50.com/adobe-ceo-shantanu-narayen-explains-why-the-company-had-to-transform/.

12. Google Trend Search (2019). 20 June 2019: https://trends.google.com/trends/explore?date=all&q=%22customer%20success%20manager%22.

13. LinkedIn.com (2019). 20 June 2019: https://www.linkedin.com/jobs/search/?f_TPR=r2592000&keywords=customer%20success& location=Worldwide&locationId=OTHERS.worldwide/.

14. Gainsight (2019). The State of the Customer Success Profession 2019, May 2019. Retrieved from: https://www.gainsight.com/press/release/new-study-powered-by-linkedin-data-reveals-customer-success-growing-736-among-top-10-fastest-growing-professions/.

15. Gainsight (2018). How Microsoft Is Building the World's Largest Customer Success Team, 19 April 2019. Posted on YouTube: https://www.youtube.com/watch?v=L5ZzugfmmmU.

16. ChannelFutures (2018). The Doyle Report: Customer Success Programs Contribute to Rise in Recurring Revenue for Cisco, Partners, 3 March 2018. Retrieved from: https://www.channelfutures.com/strategy/the-doyle-report-customer-success-programs-contribute-to-rise-in-recurring-revenue-for-cisco-partners.

17. Cisco, The Network, Cisco's Technology News Site (2019). Executive Biography, Maria Martinez, EVP and Chief Customer Experience Officer, 20 June 2019. Retrieved from: https://newsroom.cisco.com/execbio-detail?articleId=1922006.

18. Zuora, Gold, C. (2019). The Subscription Economy Index™, March 2019. Retrieved from: https://www.zuora.com/resource/subscription-economy-index/.

19. Mehta, N., Steinman, D., and Murphy, L. (2016). *Customer Success: How Innovative Companies are Reducing Churn and Growing Recurring Revenue.* Hoboken, New Jersey: Wiley.

20. Microtrends (2019). Salesforce, Inc Market Cap 2006–2019 | CRM, 21 June 2019. Retrieved from: https://www.macrotrends.net/stocks/charts/CRM/salesforce,-inc/market-cap.

21. KeyBanc Capital Markets, Technology Group (2018). SaaS Survey Results – 10th Annual. Retrieved from: https://www.key.com/businesses-institutions/industry-expertise/library-saas-resources.jsp.

22. Porter, M.E. and Heppelmann, J.E. (2015). How Smart, Connected Products Are Transforming Companies, October 2015. Retrieved from: https://hbr.org/2015/10/how-smart-connected-products-are-transforming-companies.

23. McClaffferty, A. (2015). Customer Success: The Best Kept Secret of Hyper-growth Startups, May 2015. Retrieved from: https://www.forbes.com/sites/alexmcclafferty/2015/05/18/customer-success/#74d8aeec777a.

24. Reichheld, F. and Schefter, P. (2000). The economics of e-loyalty. *Harvard Business Review* (May 2000). Retrieved from: https://hbswk.hbs.edu/archive/the-economics-of-e-loyalty.

25. Gainsight (2017). The Essential Guide to Company-wide Customer Success: Customer Success Maturity Model. Retrieved from: https://www.gainsight.com/guides/the-essential-guide-to-company-wide-customer-success/.

26. Miller, M., Vonwiller, B., Weed, P., and McKinsey & Company (2016). Grow Fast or Die Slow: Focusing on Customer Success to Drive Growth. Retrieved from: https://www.mckinsey.com/industries/high-tech/our-insights/grow-fast-or-die-slow-focusing-on-customer-success-to-drive-growth.

2 | Defining the Customer Success Manager Role

Customer Success is the business methodology of ensuring your customers achieve their desired outcomes while using your product or service. Customer Success Management is the process of proactively orchestrating and managing toward your customer's achievement of their desired outcomes. It aims to align client and vendor goals for mutually beneficial results. It logically follows then, that: "A Customer Success Manager is the qualified individual that engages with the customer, acutely assesses their needs, strategically aligns the use of your products or services to achieve those needs, and ensures that the customer attains their expected outcomes by tactically and proactively taking actions all along the way."

Goals: Increase Retention, Reduce Churn, Drive Growth

As a Customer Success Manager, *retention* is the most crucial thing you will be measured on. Technically, retention means the rate at which you keep your customers over a certain period and the revenue associated with your customer contracts. Retention is not just the act of keeping a customer. It is a process that starts with Sales but lands mostly on you, the CSM, to foster the customer to be successful with your product or service. Your purpose, simply stated, is to help a customer stay your customer.

Why? Because in the digital subscription-based age, the relationship can sometimes terminate with a click of a button. The cost of acquiring new customers can be expensive, and customer retention is a sign of the financial strength of your organization. Therefore, from the beginning of the customer relationship, you want to make sure that your customers are educated, engaged, and active because a highly engaged customer means high customer retention.

The opposite of retention is churn. In the subscription and Customer Success world, "churn" is a four-letter word! Churn means a customer has decided they no longer want to be your customer. It is the complete opposite of retention, and it is your primary responsibility as a CSM to prevent it.

The Customer Success Manager is the frontline of modern organizations and often the individual operationally responsible for preventing customer churn. In SaaS companies, the CSM's primary charter is to ensure the renewal event is essentially a non-event. CSMs are also responsible for building customer loyalty, improving satisfaction, raising customer advocacy, increasing product adoption, and driving growth and revenue expansion. CSMs are expected to do it all! It's a vast scope of responsibility. As a result, most CSMs are constantly challenged to balance all their duties and objectives on a day-to-day basis.

Fortunately, Customer Success leaders are learning to prioritize the charters of their CS teams. In a 2019 Gainsight survey that benchmarked the Customer Success category, more than 900 respondents shared the top three most important objectives of their customer success team (Figure 2.1).

Surprisingly, *improving the Net Promoter Score (NPS)* was not even in the top five, and *improving customer satisfaction* was at the bottom. Pause and think about that for a moment. Although customer success leaders care about NPS and CSAT (Customer Satisfaction surveys), their primary focus is on generating higher customer retention rates, revenue growth, and improved product adoption. Fortunately, the CSM is in the perfect position to drive towards these objectives.

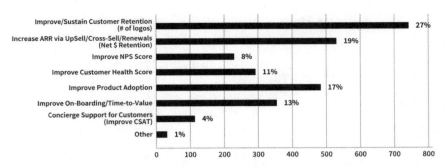

Figure 2.1 Gainsight 2019 Customer Success industry benchmark Survey.

The Consumption Gap

In his book, *Complexity Avalanche,* J.B. Wood acutely describes a core challenge facing today's technology companies, and therefore Customer Success Managers. Wood states that "if your end customers can't figure out how to use your product or they can't get it to work in their network, or they can't change their business process to adapt to its features, it has little or no value to them."[1] He goes on to explain that "the difference between the value of the product *could* provide to the customer and the value it actually *does* provide is what we call the 'consumption gap' (Figure 2.2). The ultimate goal today is to enable customers and their businesses to get full value out of the product."

Figure 2.2 first aims to point out what is possible with your product versus how your customer is actually using it. The assumption is that the more your customers leverage and use your product to attain their desired outcomes, the less likely they will churn. The goal, of course, is to shrink that gap over time. The second inference of this graphic is that your product and development teams are busy at work creating new features and enhancements, thereby widening the gap with every new release. CSMs work from within an often-fluctuating consumption gap.

The symphony of movement within the consumption gap creates a number of opportunities. For example, new product features often create different and better use-cases for existing customers to derive additional value. New features can also mean new upsell and expansion opportunities

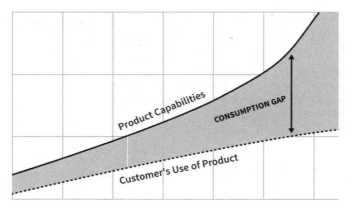

Figure 2.2   The consumption gap (Wood 2009).

if priced separately from the base product. A piece of advice: you should always be working for a company that is continuously innovating and raising the bar on what is possible with your product. Assuming that is the case, one of the most challenging aspects of being a CSM at a fast-growing and innovative company is keeping up with all of the advancing product capabilities. To serve your customers properly, you must know your product extremely well. Only then will you be able to close the consumption gap to the benefit of your customer and your company.

The Customer Success Equation

Customer Success is the belief that "We only succeed if you succeed." When you can demonstrate to your customers the value of their engagement by helping them attain their desired Customer Outcomes (CO), they will more eagerly renew, expand, and advocate on your behalf. Customers are truly the sleeping giant of your revenue stream, and your customer success efforts have the potential to create a growth engine entirely cultivated from existing customers. However, Customer Success is only a portion of the success equation. Customer Experience (CX), is a separate discipline that develops happy and satisfied customers. However, what happens when your happy customer doesn't attain their desired outcomes?

$$CS = CX + CO$$

Customer Success is the combination of the customer's experience as they attain their desired outcomes. When you have one without the other, the results are not optimal. The customer must derive value from your product or service. Customer Success is not about customer satisfaction. It is not about customer delight. It is about delivering value with a wonderful experience.

Figure 2.3 is a 2×2 illustration that helps visualize the relationship between Customer Experience and Customer Outcomes.

The horizontal (*x*-axis) reflects the measure of delivered outcome to the customer's expectations. The vertical (*y*-axis) demonstrates the degree of positive experience from the customer's perspective. As with most 2×2 management consulting charts, you always want to be in the upper-right corner. In this case, you've delivered on your brand promise, helped the customer attain their desired outcome, and have done so by giving them an awesome experience all along the way. A customer in any other quadrant is at risk of churn.

The upper-left quadrant is an interesting one. It represents customers that have a great experience engaging with your company (e.g. great people, amazing team, easy to work with, or highly responsive) but it has failed to deliver the business results the customer expected. Customers in this quadrant are often misclassified as "healthy." They may even give you a 9 or

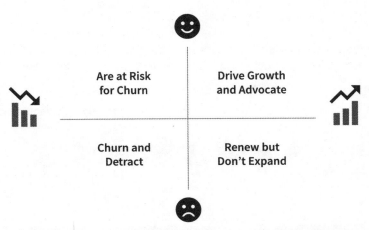

Figure 2.3   Customer Experience and Customer Outcomes. (Gainsight)

10 on an NPS survey. However, in this case, the sentiment signal is a false positive.

Similarly, customers in the lower-right quadrant attained their desired business results, but they didn't have an optimal experience with your company. While they may not churn, they likely won't expand their engagement with you. If their experience was poor, they will begin looking to your competitors, who all claim they can deliver equal, if not better results, and likely for less money and with a far better experience.

The Net Promoter Score (NPS)

A Net Promoter Score, or NPS, is a core measurement or method that most companies use to measure overall customer satisfaction. It shows customer health and loyalty. It is also a lead indicator or prediction of future product adoption and growth. Most of you have probably participated in one or two NPS surveys, either online, in an email, or over the phone. The method is to ask, "How likely are you to recommend our product to a friend or colleague?" The answers are on a scale from zero to ten.

Answers from zero to six, are considered pretty unhappy customers. These are called "Detractors." They can "churn" easily, and hinder growth by sharing their feelings with other colleagues, customers, or online. Detractors can give your brand a bad reputation.

Scores from seven to eight are called "Passives." That means they are satisfied, but not completely committed to your product. They are indifferent and are susceptible to competitors who may make them an offer they can't refuse.

The top scores of nine and ten are your "Promoters." These customers are loyal and enthusiastic about your product, and will most likely renew, or buy more. They are also going to refer you to other people.

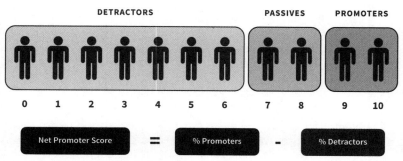

A snapshot of customer satisfaction.

We have established that your goal as a Customer Success Manager is to deliver customer outcomes with a great experience. However, there is one stakeholder that is missing from the $CS = CX + CO$ equation: your company. Recall, customer retention and increasing revenues are the two most essential objectives of Customer Success teams from a CS-leader's perspective. As such, there is a strong likelihood that you, as a CSM, will be measured by customer retention rates and revenue growth that is derived from the portfolio of customers you manage. Simply put, you want your customers to remain customers and buy more stuff from you. You are helping to deliver the variables for success not only for your customers but also for your company. However, how do you balance delivering success for your customers while also attaining your company metrics?

During an internal company-wide gathering, our leader, Gainsight CEO Nick Mehta responded to a similar question about our investor, stakeholder, and strategic objectives. His answer was magnificent and is paraphrased here: "In order to have the opportunity to help our customers attain their success, we also have to be successful in business. Otherwise, we won't have the opportunity to engage new and existing customers. It's a golden circle of sorts. You can't have one without the other." Nick was spot on. Customer Success is a vital element in this new way of thinking. The way a customer feels about their experience at the end of their contract in light of the results you helped them produce can fuel growth and more opportunity to help more customers.

What Customer Success Management is Not

While we have addressed what a Customer Success Manager is, it is equally important to know what it is not. We learned earlier that there could be a mountain of various expectations placed on CSMs. Figure 2.4 illustrates the unique space that Customer Success Managers are taking in the modern organization. There can also be an overlap in skills and responsibilities that make the CSM appear like a newer version of support or account management, for example.

It is helpful to clarify the definition of a Customer Success Manager further, by contrasting what a Customer Success Manager does not, or rather should not, entail.

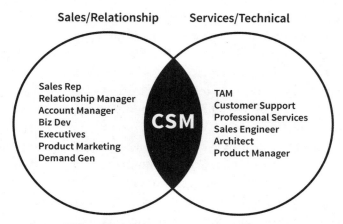

Figure 2.4   What Customer Success Management is/is not (Gainsight).

Not Customer Support

Customer Support is hugely important to the customer ecosystem. However, it is mostly transactional, focused on break/fix interactions, and is almost always reactive in nature. In the foundational CS industry book, *Customer Success: How Innovative Companies are Reducing Churn and Growing Recurring Revenue*, Nick Mehta and Dan Steinman keenly acknowledge "both organizations [support and customer success] are 100% needed to be effective as a company. The admonition here is to be mindful that they are not designed to accomplish the same goals."[2]

Customer Success focuses on the longitudinal relationship, not the transactional one. Applying the Pareto principle, commonly known as the 80/20 rule, 80% of CSM activity should be proactive, and 20% reactive. If that formula is inverse at your company, it's not Customer Success. You and your company's leaders need to be honest and call it what it is: escalated Customer Support. Simply renaming an organization as "Customer Success" will not yield different behaviors nor different outcomes.

Not Account Management/Sales

Sales and Account Management engagements are, at their core, financially driven, heavily incentivized, and mostly transaction-based. Importantly, the individuals in these critical roles typically only engage at account-level milestones, such as contract renewals, paid professional services engagements via Statements of Work (SOW), or expansion opportunities. While their methods have elements of relationship-building and they help to align your company's products to solve customer challenges, the pinnacle of the Sales and Account Manager engagement is attained when the prospect or customer completes the commercial transaction. In all likelihood, sales won't re-engage again until there is a new sales opportunity in sight.

The CSM, on the other hand, must foster the relationship throughout the customer's journey, ensuring the customer achieves their expected goal. We will keep saying it many times: when a customer attains their desired outcome while having a great experience, they will inevitably buy more from you. While it may not be your primary duty to manage the commercial aspects of your customer, you are indeed doing all of the heavy lifting to make any future transactions justifiable. As a CSM, whether you realize it or not, you are constantly selling your solution through the results it produces. Your successful efforts will lead to more commercial transactions in the form of renewal, an expansion, a referral, or all three.

A Career or a Springboard to a Real Profession?

It is absolutely true that Customer Success Managers often launch into other roles after "putting in their time." There is a reason for this phenomenon. CSMs are some of the most capable people on the face of the planet. Yes, we are a little biased. However, the simple truth is that the role affords you a rare opportunity to learn and understand how your customers think and how they work with your products at a truly intimate level of exposure not typically granted to Marketing, Sales, Support, or Product. As a result, you become a sort of hot commodity inside and outside of your company. Growth opportunities abound for really effective and successful CSMs. We have seen and heard of Customer Success Managers moving into literally every department – Training, Marketing, Product, Analytics, Operations, Consulting, Professional Services, HR, and more. We have also seen CSMs, perfectly happy to remain as individual contributors, managing their dynamic portfolio of customers.

Skilled people can advance very fast, especially where experienced CS professionals are in short supply. That is pure supply and demand economics. We even know of a few people that have gone from Customer Success Manager to Chief Customer Officer in a relatively short period of time. Of course, there is always another side of the coin. The visibility of Customer Success continues to increase every day. Inside the companies that have a successful CS practice, there is a growing level of attention that comes onto the function, even to the individual CSM. If you are okay with a job where the CEO asks, in good or bad circumstances, "Who is the CSM on that account?" you'll be just fine. It is the nature and rising importance of the function. And that's a great thing if you are an aspirational person.

For the record, we ascribe to the notion that the Customer Success Manager role can be a great catalyst for other opportunities. We both have launched into different positions and management roles after being individual contributing CSMs with our own assigned portfolio of customers. We didn't leave the function because we didn't like it. Instead, it was a passion for the opportunity to improve the profession, the Customer Success Manager function, and its impact on our customers and the greater CS community that drove us to pursue related opportunities. Hence the question "Is a Customer Success Manager, a career or simply a springboard to a real profession?" To answer, we asked industry icon Jon Herstein, Chief Customer Officer at Box, to provide his perspective on this specific topic.

Customer Success Manager as a Profession

By Jon Herstein, Chief Customer Officer at Box

Since the dawn of the Customer Success age, the role of the Customer Success Manager has grown and evolved along with the progression of SaaS. While this evolution is still underway, it's becoming increasingly clear that being a CSM is much more than a waystation to another career destination.

One of the key questions for customer success organizations has been, "What is the exact role of the CSM, and how is that role defined, measured and valued?" Because of the maturation of the profession, that has been a challenging question to answer. A parallel question has been equally difficult: "Is this a profession?"

In my organization, I have encouraged the career mobility of CSMs into numerous other roles, including Consulting, Product Management, Sales, and Marketing. While this approach has been rewarding for individuals and valuable for the organization, it is still uncertain if CSMs consider it a career or simply a job along the way to something "better."

Customer Success Manager is a rewarding but challenging job. It requires the application of a symphony of skills and a high level of tenacity. When you're in the CSM role, a lot of other jobs can look very attractive. Wouldn't it be fun to help build the product rather than apologize for it? What if I could get paid like a salesperson and work less than I do today? Is there really a two-drink minimum in Marketing? Even CS Operations could be a great way to leverage my CSM experience without talking to customers all day long!

For the organization, it makes complete sense to recruit Customer Success Managers into other company roles. Having deep, customer-facing people in positions where they build, market, and sell the product means better solution and product–market fit, resulting in more satisfied customers. Plus, the ramp-up time of an experienced CSM compared to an outside hire is accelerated.

So, what's the problem with this? There's a blanket assumption that you wouldn't want to be a CSM for very long. This assumption leads to high turnover in the relationships we're trying so hard to cultivate and nurture. That, in turn, decreases the depth of relationships we have with our customers, our knowledge of their pain points and planned business outcomes, and thus, the value we (as CSMs) add to

(continued)

(continued)

the relationship. All of which leads to the customer asking, "Why have I had three different CSMs in two years?"

Increasingly, however, Customer Success Managers are beginning to realize that being a CSM isn't simply a job on the way to another, better job. It can be and is a career. That isn't to say that every person who accepts a CSM job will become a career Customer Success Manager. Nonetheless, there is a clear set of attributes that consistently show up in the CSMs who come to this career realization. They are interested in building long-term relationships with their customers. They are less motivated by transactional rewards (commissions and spiffs) than by true customer success. At the same time, they want to be valued, rewarded, and recognized for their work, so increasing compensation and titles are important. They are respected and trusted by their customers for the valuable insight and "challenger" mindset they bring to every discussion. They hone their craft as professional Customer Success Managers, identifying patterns in their work, strengthening their advocacy on behalf of their customers, and insisting that they are a co-equal partner to sales and renewal professionals on the account team.

When all of these traits come together in a single person, they can take on more complex, strategic, and higher-value customers. Their earning potential climbs as a result, and promotions with titles such as "Customer Success Director" and "Customer Success Executive" become the norm, rather than the exception.

While software professions like Product Management, Sales, Consulting, and others have been around for decades, the Customer Success arena is still relatively new. It's pioneer days for those Customer Success Managers who have already decided that being a CSM is their "calling." They will thrive at the forefront of the subscription-driven Customer Success movement and they will become the first generation of senior leaders who "grew up" (professionally) as Customer Success practitioners.

Today's CCOs come from varied backgrounds. Tomorrow's CCOs will almost certainly be former Customer Success Managers who will run their organizations with the benefit of their hard-won experience as professional Customer Success Managers.

Endnotes

1. Wood, J.B. (2009). *Complexity Avalanche*. USA: State Point B Inc.
2. Mehta, N., Steinman, D., and Murphy, L. (2016). *Customer Success: How Innovative Companies are Reducing Churn and Growing Recurring Revenue*. Hoboken, New Jersey: Wiley.

PART II

The Core Skills of a Great CSM

3

A Day in the Life of a Customer Success Manager

We have discussed the imperatives of Customer Success and the purpose of the Customer Success Manager role. Now, it's time to start describing what a typical day in the life of a Customer Success Manager looks like. It is important to note that CSMs may be asked to perform to different metrics and objectives based on their company. And this means their activities may vary from company to company. Nevertheless, there are strong commonalities across all business segments that employ a properly leveraged CS team.

Putting Customer Success into Practice

Below is a summary of the main elements you'll encounter as a CSM. It's a true and real glimpse into a day in the life of a CS professional. It is also instructive. Even if you are currently a CSM, you may find new tips and tricks to help you navigate through your day. Admittedly, it's not comprehensive, but it is intended to capture the most critical mileposts of a CSM throughout a typical day, week, or month.

Day in the life of a CSM:

1. **Check your calendar before you do anything else.** That's correct. Check your calendar first, not your inbox. Your calendar should accurately reflect appointments that have been scheduled prior, and you'll want to have your day and critical appointments registered top-of-mind before you start your day off. It is also an opportunity for you to reprioritize any non-essential meetings.

2. **Review your proactive to-do list.** Review your *proactive* to-do list. Don't check your inbox first. Start with a list that should consist of items you've deferred from previous days, important date-triggered events such as customer renewals, upcoming business reviews, and anything else that requires your attention *today*.

3. **Check your inbound messages** (email, Slack, or other messaging systems). Certainly, this is to each person's individual preference. However, we strongly advise you to not check your inbound messages until you've reviewed your calendar and to-do list. You'll have a much better chance of regulating your priorities *before* you open your inbox. As you may very well know, your messages can be wrought with often over-amplified demands for your immediate attention on subjects that can and should wait. Of course, you will also discover customer or internal escalations and other influences that may require you to shift your day. Just be cautious and self-disciplined as you do. Another suggestion is to put self-imposed constraints on how much time you spend reading and responding to messages.

4. **New customers.** On days where you've been assigned a new customer, you'll want to take some specific steps before and immediately after your first encounter with them.
   - Using an alert notification system, like Google Alerts, set an alert of the company name that has been assigned to you. The more you are informed about various happenings with your customers, the better you will be able to advise them. You also want to learn in real-time about potentially impactful news like your customer getting acquired (a risk to your relationship) or your customer acquiring another company (a potential expansion opportunity).
   - Update all of the known contacts, specifically email addresses, phone numbers, and current titles, in your Customer Relationship

Management (CRM) system. Denote them based on their persona and level of influence or decision-making capacities.

- Draft an org-chart of your customer's reporting structure of known contacts. As a bonus, create an influence chart that shows the decision-making hierarchy and connection points of all known customer contacts. Collaborate with Sales on this. Spend a little time on LinkedIn researching how customer contacts are connected with people within your organization.
- Connect with all your customer contacts via LinkedIn. Be sure to send them a simple personal message when doing so. You will need this channel in the future for a variety of reasons, including the sourcing of new sales and expansion opportunities, understanding your customer's scope of influence, and the occasional "like" on a post or comment to remind them you care.
- Ascertain from the Sales Rep what the customer's imperative is for engaging your company. What business problems are they trying to solve? What expectations do they have in terms of timelines and measurable outcomes? You'll eventually have to validate all of them with your customer, but it is far better to state your current understanding than to expect your customers to repeat themselves, having just completed the sales cycle.

5. **Value discussions.** Every engagement should be a value discussion that helps your customer move closer to their desired outcome. The engagements may involve sharing best practices, advising on change-management tactics, educating the customer on existing or new product features, or diving deep on a specific business challenge that can be solved with your product. Value discussions represent the majority of your live conversations or meetings with your customers.

6. **Success planning.** Success planning is a mechanism to capture and track objectives and timelines that have been mutually agreed between you and your customer to ensure progress toward your customer's desired outcomes. We will this topic in greater depth in Chapter 11.

7. **Executive Business Reviews (EBRs).** Conducting regular business reviews shows your customers that they are moving toward the objectives and targets they have defined with you. You want to establish a precedent from the beginning that you and your company desire to engage at the executive level regularly for their best interests. The most important message delivered during EBRs is that you are working toward the customer's return on their investment with you. We will cover more on EBRs in Chapter 8.

8. **CS team meeting.** Always prepare for any meeting you attend, including your own CS team meetings. Make sure you are familiar with all internal updates, new procedures, revised playbooks, new use-cases, or refreshed best practices. Don't squander the time you have with your peers. Learn from each other. Share your customer stories (good and bad) and do something fun for a few minutes at the beginning of each meeting.

9. **Risk/Escalation (internal).** Besides renewals reviews, your next most important internal meetings or actions will be dedicated to managing risks. At the highest level, the categories of risk include Implementation, Sentiment, Support, Product, Company, and Renewal.

   ▪ **Implementation risk:** it's not uncommon for one of your assigned customers to have challenges during implementation or onboarding. Onboarding issues are not limited to new customers. You may have an existing customer engage your professional services team for some additional enablement or custom configuration via a formal Statement of Work (SOW). This agreement states how the product will be implemented, configured, and what resources will be required by both the customer and the vendor. A schedule or timeline can also guide it. As a CSM, you should always closely monitor and intervene as early as possible during this phase. Otherwise, the issues or, worse, the customer's negative sentiments will inevitably carry forward post-implementation, making it more difficult for you to advance the customer toward their objectives.

   ▪ **Sentiment risk:** there are two types of sentiment. The first reflects your customer's sentiment about your company and product. This is usually recorded in an NPS survey. The second reflects your assessment of how the customer really feels about your company and product. Ultimately, the latter is a subjective judgment about the risk of future renewal. At any point in time, you should always be able to answer this question, "If my customer's renewal were tomorrow, would they be eager and happy to sign on for at least another year?" Also, don't be afraid to ask the customer that same question. Be prepared to listen and learn no matter what their answer is.

   ▪ **Support risk:** Support is one of the most critical and often under-appreciated functions in a company. We LOVE our Support team, and you should love yours too. When a customer is struggling with anything related to support, be very careful not to come in heavy-handed but always with a spirit of collaboration. Your Support team is unceasingly bombarded every single day with issues and challenges that almost always stem from product gaps, data integration or interface problems, or, far too often, a customer's lack of knowledge and training in the product itself. You should have thresholds pre-established that can automatically notify you when there are extraordinary circumstances. Circumstances such as too many new support cases reported over a particular time period, too many cases open at once, too many Priority-1 or critical cases, or too long waiting for a resolution.

- Be sure not to mistake "no support cases" as a positive thing. It can be a signal that the customer is completely disengaged from the product. If you need to escalate a customer's issue, don't just toss it over the proverbial fence. Always ask your Support colleagues questions like "What can I do to help expedite the resolution? Do I need to engage the product engineering team? Do I need to engage leadership? How can I be of service to you during this situation?" Take ownership of rallying resources and keeping all involved through regular communication, but be careful not to perform the support activity yourself. It's a trap many great CSMs fall into because of their intimate knowledge of the product and their customers. We have seen far too many CS teams performing as an escalation-support organization instead of proactively driving customer value and expanding the business.

- **Product risk:** always approach the Engineering team with a true spirit of collaboration, as you do with Support. Often, product risks are really about product gaps and petitioning for expedited enhancement requests or bug fixes. Don't bring anecdotal stories of one customer's challenges. Think about it for a moment. If you have 30 CSM teammates and each of them has at least two active product issues raised independently with the product team, that's 60 separate issues that have to be triaged, prioritized, evaluated, and managed. All of that is time away from product development that could be used instead to create the enhancements and fix the bugs you've each independently raised. Instead, consider aggregating issues within your CS team first. Let the data be your bull-horn. If 20 of those 60 issues were all related to the same fundamental product gap, you could literally carry the message back to the Product team that sounds something like this: "20 customers, representing $2.8M in ARR, with $1M up for renewal this quarter, are at risk due to a common product issue." Then provide some qualifications on the impact if the issue isn't fixed in a specific time period. That is a stronger, more compelling message than each CSM carrying their individual stories. As a CSM team, you must also be good stewards of your company's resources, especially your precious product and engineering teams.

- **Company risk:** company risk includes events mostly out of your control, such as the departure of any of your primary customer contacts, like a customer decision-maker or adoption-champion. It can also include changes in your customer's market or shifts in their industry, such as acquisitions. In some more dire circumstances, it could be the financial instability of your customer in the form of late payments. The focus of this aspect is about mitigating the risks by having various playbooks ready to be executed at a moment's notice. On a more positive note, almost all company risks include an opportunity. If you've helped to make your customer's decision-maker very successful, it's not uncommon for them to jump to greener pastures and take on new and exciting roles at bigger and better companies. It often translates into a hot new sales opportunity that was derived entirely from all your excellent work prior. The same holds for acquisitions. Consider them both risk and opportunity. In all cases, always set realistic expectations and try to overcommunicate.

10. **Renewals review (internal).** From a company perspective, this is probably the most important meeting of your day or week. You must have complete and full visibility of all your customers up for renewal in the current quarter and especially in the current month. More importantly, you must know with the highest level of certainty the probability of each customer renewing because you don't want your name attached to any surprise customer churns. We will dive more into managing renewals in Chapter 8.

11. **One-on-one with your manager.** Another critical internal meeting is your sync-meeting with your direct manager. These should happen every month or two. While these meetings often devolve into tactical and customer-specific discussions, you'll want to advocate to reserve a portion of each meeting to discuss your professional development needs, your career goals, trajectory, and your standing as a contributing team member. Great CSMs are eager to solicit and receive feedback about their performance and to seek advice and guidance. If you've been a CSM for several years, it's easy to fall into complacency, which

allows bad habits to form. Every company and every manager has a particular style and way of carrying out customer success disciplines. If you need this time to discuss a customer-related situation, come well prepared and provide your manager with advance notice and context so they can be more helpful during what is likely a 15–30-minute meeting.

12. **Promoter and advocacy request.** We know that when happy customers are achieving their desired outcomes, they are the only ones genuinely willing to refer your company, product, or service to friends, family, or colleagues. Customer advocacy starts on the first day of the Customer Lifecycle with the intent of creating a Customer Advocate. You will read more about building an effective advocacy program in Chapter 12.

13. **One-to-many outreaches.** Learning to work efficiently is critical to your success as a CSM. Whether you have five customers or a thousand, you should leverage technology and automation platforms to help extend your reach. You will learn more about this topic in Chapter 10.

14. **Product training.** CSMs usually spend all day, every day with customers. Assisting customers, training customers, coaching and advising customers, and helping customers get value . . . out of *the product*. CSMs ultimately help customers solve their business problems, using *the product*. They are also the people often closest to customers, and see how they use, or want to use the product. If that is true, then it makes perfect sense that the highest priority of the CSM is to help improve the product and the outcomes it facilitates and delivers to customers. Therefore, becoming intimately familiar with your company's products and solutions is vital to your success as a CSM. Customer success is critical, but customers will not be happy without a great product. You have an obligation to help improve it. Simply said, everything points back to the product. No company in SaaS can survive without having a good product. In fact, if you want to do more than survive, you have to have the best product. Even further, trying to convince a customer that they can find value in a sub-par product that doesn't fit their needs in the first place, goes against everything that CS stands for. How can you make them a success with a product that does not fit or work well for them? It is on you to become product knowledgeable. You own your calendar, so make it a priority also to own your learning paths to greater product expertise. There will be more covered on this subject in Chapter 4.

Being a Customer Success Manager – A Personal Testimonial

Now that you've seen a glimpse of what a potential day might look like for a CSM, we believe it is equally important to provide you with a first-hand account from one of the most effective CSMs we know. Easton Taylor has been in a variety of Customer Success related roles since 2012. We are fortunate to call him our colleague. We have seen his mastery of the profession in action for many years now. We truly admire his tenacity, dedication, and style. As such, we've asked him to share his CS journey with you. Specifically, to provide some of the essentials of his success as a CSM.

On Being a Customer Success Manager

By Easton Taylor, Director of Customer Success at Gainsight

Becoming a CSM was one of the most beneficial decisions I've made in my career. What surprised me the most in the two first years was how many facets of an organization CSMs actually encounter – from Sales to Product to Marketing to Support to Services to the Executive Suite. It's why I love this role. There is always an opportunity to learn something new every day.

One of the most important things you can do is to become as intimate with your customer as possible. Take a little time out of each day to purposefully learn about your customers and their companies. It should include visiting the company website, sitting through a demonstration of their product, reading through their financial statements if available, researching them on LinkedIn, Google News, and other sources, getting to know their competition, understanding the industry they serve, and so forth. This extra level of effort allows you to foster a sincere appreciation for your customer's business. The goal is to establish a trusted advisor relationship with the customers you serve. They will not just look to you as someone that can help them with the product, but also as someone that understands and can better advise them in their domain. What an amazing feeling.

The responsibility of managing customers to their desired outcomes is significant. It requires a host of skills that every CSM will need to flex on a daily basis: preparation, communication, prioritization, time management, empathy, and follow-up, to name a few. However, preparation and follow-up are the most critical. A big part of the role is interacting with your customers through cadence calls, EBRs, strategic best practice sessions, training, product roadmap reviews, and more. Before any customer interaction, ask yourself these questions:

"Have I thoroughly thought about the client's needs and expectations for this meeting?"

"Who will be joining the meeting and are the appropriate roles assigned?"

"Is there anything that I can provide the customer before the meeting to make our time more efficient?"

"What does success look like for this meeting?"

After the meeting or call is over, switch immediately to follow-up. All that preparation can quickly go to waste if you don't follow-up with highlights from the discussion, summarizing clear and actionable next steps, identifying owners of those next steps, and providing related content and any training materials. Stay organized and diligent so that your follow-up results in progress for the customer toward their desired goals.

Most of your remaining time will be spent on problem-solving. In a perfect world, your customers would purchase your product for exactly what that product was built to do, and nothing more. In this scenario, the Customer Success profession wouldn't exist. Thankfully, customers are far more creative in finding new use-cases and challenges. That requires you to solve unexpected business problems with the product and features you have in-hand. You can't just tell the customer that you'll put in an enhancement request. You have to help solve the immediate problem. While this may sound a little intimidating, it is one of the best aspects of being a CSM. Truly, not one situation is ever the same.

(continued)

(continued)

It produces a freshness within a job that is rare to find elsewhere. At times, you will need to be firm with your customers and tell them what they are doing is inadvisable, or outright wrong. It's your responsibility to ensure you guide them in the right direction and they don't make avoidable mistakes. Of course, do so with a dose of humility and confidence.

This role is remarkably rewarding. I personally struggle with the age-old question, "What is my purpose in life?" I've realized it is to help people. I know I'm not helping to cure cancer, but my life didn't take that path, and I'm okay with that. I am grateful for this profession because being a Customer Success Manager has allowed me to help people solve problems that they are facing, help them get questions to answers they are pondering, help make their teams be more efficient, help them get a raise or promotion, or simply help ease their frustration.

If any of the above resonates with you and you are thinking about joining this profession, my advice is to jump in head-first and enjoy the ride.

As Easton said, a CSM's role is remarkably rewarding. However, you want to bring your "A" game to this burgeoning industry. With your skills and passion, you will stand out from the other CSMs. This combination will lead you in any direction you want to go – even the C-suite.

The Three Core CSM Competencies

There are many skills you need in order to be a great CSM. These include traditional soft skills like relationship building and self-awareness. You will also need baseline skills required of most Customer Success professionals, like preparing for executive reviews, understanding the Customer Lifecycle and Journey Map, building and using Health Scores, mitigating customer risks, and managing renewals and driving advocacy, to name a few. Lastly, the best CSMs attain a high degree of product expertise and proficiency. All these skills can be categorized into three core competencies that you need to develop over your career to become great at your role.

Within the CS community, leaders are finding that certain general attributes will aid you as a Customer Success Manager. Given how cross-functional a CSM's role is, it's no surprise that you will be expected to have a wide array of skills at your disposal. To make it more actionable, we will cover the three core competencies that differentiate great CSMs from good ones.

Skill 1: Knowledge Mastery

The first competency is mastery of the knowledge of your industry, category, and product. Subject matter experience gives you credibility as a trusted advisor to your customer. While having experience in the industry that your target customer belongs to is valuable, your expertise in the product will make you stand out. A CSM with experience in the category can empathize with what your product's users experience, day in and day out. It also helps them talk credibly about best practices and trends in the category. Lastly, having technical knowledge of your product or service is an excellent addition to your professional repertoire, especially if you can identify its differentiators and competition. Your company is depending on you to know their product and service to answer questions and concerns from the purchaser. Any prior product experience from a role at another company, even a competitor, amplifies your current product knowledge. You will be able to compare and contrast use-cases for the customer, assuring them they made the right choice. We will dive into this first critical competency in greater detail in Chapter 4.

Skill 2: Problem-Solving Ability

The second competency, being a problem solver, is highly prized in any business field. Customers are looking to you as their trusted advisor to consult with them on what is the best way to solve their issues. That means you must understand the business challenges that may be unique to them.

The way you get to understand their business challenges is by asking a ton of relevant questions.

Another vital skill is preparing for every engagement with your customers – don't take anything for granted. Advising, alone, is not enough. You must have the ability to take action. Customers don't always know the best ways your product solves their business challenges. That is why they look to you. Another great skill to develop is the "challenger mindset" and learning to say "no" when your customers want to continue their bad processes. There is nothing beneficial to you or your customer when you allow them to wander off the best practices track while using your product.

The last step to enhancing your abilities as a problem solver is learning to prioritize which customers get your time and attention. Prioritizing means answering the right customer at the right time with the right message. We go into more detail in Chapter 6.

Skill 3: Building Relationships with Your Customers

Of all the skills that you can acquire as a CSM, becoming more empathetic is probably one of the most important that you should develop. Customer Success is known as a "human-first" concept and endeavor. As a CSM, you must reach out beyond yourself and place yourself in your customer's shoes. Knowing the product, industry, having the technical knowledge, and problem-solving are well and good individual skills. Together they show impressive competency.

The real power of your expertise lies in understanding your customers and how all of those competencies impact them. Once you connect to your customers, you begin to build a relationship with them. The trust you create through clear communications during your interactions enhances your influence as a trusted advisor. In that way, your impact and influence as a CSM has the potential for a virtuous cycle of advocacy, simply out of doing your job really well. We will cover this important competency in Chapter 5.

•••

As you progress, this book will broaden these concepts for you. You will also find tips on how you can build and utilize these techniques. Be assured that at the beginning of your career, you do not have to be proficient in each one at equal levels. Instead, you should see yourself as well-rounded with broad generalized knowledge. Customer Success Managers are already super-human. Becoming a subject-matter expert CSM will take time and experience.

4 | The CSM Skills Required in an Ever-Evolving Business World

In this chapter, we will focus on knowledge mastery, which includes attaining proficiency in your industry, category, and product. Knowledge mastery is particularly important for you as a Customer Success Manager, especially if your company's product is in the early stages of maturation. In those formative years, a broad understanding of the industries and category your company serves will enable you to see associated pain-points, how your target market is evolving, and how your product aims to solve real problems.

The ability to comprehend these subjects goes a long way toward winning over early customers. However, as your knowledge matures along with your company, you may find the need to move from a broad and general understanding, to a more focused, specialized view. This could mean becoming more technically savvy with your products and evolving your industry and domain expertise. It is also important that you find mentors and use other methods of educating yourself to become the best CSM for your company, with your products, for your customers and the industries they serve.

How to Develop Your Industry and Category Knowledge

To begin, let's give some definitions.

- A **category** is a sector of an industry that includes a cluster of companies that are solving a recognized problem within it.
- An **industry** is a slice of the economy that includes business entities, knowledge workers, products, and services.

Categories can be both horizontal and vertical and cross multiple industries. Companies with products designed for a **vertical category,** like medical devices, would not likely be active in the oil and gas industry. For instance, Veeva Systems Inc. is a cloud-computing company focused on pharmaceutical and life sciences industry applications. Veeva serves a specific vertical category. Another example is Procore, which makes project management software for the construction industry. An example of a **horizontal category** company is Salesforce. It sells software solutions for Sales Representatives across numerous industries. Customer Success is another example of a horizontal category. Our own company, Gainsight, sells a suite of customer-centric solutions including Customer Success across a wide variety of industries.

If you are new to a particular industry or category and aren't familiar with its nuances, it can be intimidating to interview for CSM jobs in those areas – and ace it. If you've passed the hurdles of getting the job, it can be difficult to excel at your role without the requisite industry knowledge. Even if you are an experienced CSM in a particular industry, you can't only rely on your past acquired knowledge either. It is equally important for industry seasoned CSMs and new CSMs to keep abreast of developments and changes to regulations and laws that might have a significant impact on the industry you're working in.

A critical tool at your disposal is certifications. Many industries and companies offer certifications focused on roles in specific industries. For example, Google provides certifications in digital marketing and the AdWords platform. If you plan to serve as a CSM in the digital marketing category, you should seriously consider earning that certification. If your company sells products and services in project management, you should consider getting certified as a Project Management Professional (PMP), an internationally recognized professional designation offered by the Project Management Institute (PMI). For CS professionals like yourselves, Gainsight offers an educational program designed specifically for the Customer Success category called Pulse+, with varying levels of advanced certifications.

Most companies will pay for their employees to get certified, either directly or via reimbursement. You should ask your human resources about professional development budget allocations and any other opportunities to advance your capabilities as a CSM.

While mastery of industry or category is necessary, it is also essential to know how people actually use your product in their daily jobs. That includes how the product is evolving for them. An exciting way for a CSM to gather information is to conduct what is called "chairside" interviews with customers. Think of chairsides as a 30–60 minute virtual or in-person session, where you sit with the customer's users, and have them walk through a typical "day in their lives." It is a brilliant way for CSMs to develop empathy for what your customers encounter on a regular basis. You will see the challenges faced in their job and how it is evolving. Understanding their jobs more intimately will equip you to better help your customers use your product to their benefit.

As we contemplated the topic of knowledge mastery, it was important for us to bring a perspective from someone that has built a CS team that demands very comprehensive industry knowledge and a high level of product expertise. We approached Eduarda Camacho, Executive Vice President, Customer Operations at PTC, a provider of digital transformation solutions. We learned that when she joined PTC, she quickly figured out that there was a need for CSMs to have deep category experience, or as she calls it "domain experience":

> Customer domain expertise is an essential competency for our Customer Success Managers. It matters in the same way that business language matters. There must be a proficiency of both to thrive as a good CSM. At PTC, we *now* know that our customer-facing resources must have knowledge of the discrete manufacturing space. They must also be aware of the related business drivers. Our strategic customers and partners value

our fluency in engineering and technical language. As we have diversified into other industries like oil and gas and medical devices, we recognized the need to speak their language too. For example, a specific fluency was needed for engaging shop floor factory stakeholders. The transformation of our approach further emphasized how important domain expertise is to our success as well as our customers'.

Mastering your industry knowledge enhances the CSM's ability to become a trusted advisor and establishes credibility. We also firmly believe our CSMs need to be product savvy to understand the use-cases and the implications to the business, not just "the points and clicks." That is especially true with customers that have more mature implementations. They tend to need a more knowledgeable CSM to drive them through product adoption-related challenges.

What we needed was different profiles: relationship, domain, and product experts. We also learned the importance of properly matching the customer to the correct profile. It must be deliberate and will vary based on the engagement. Today we have a healthy mix of high-level relationship CSMs, deep domain experts, and product-expert CSMs. We needed this mix in our business to be successful. You too might consider a similar approach with your company. More importantly, as a Customer Success professional, it should always be your desire to learn more about the customers and industry you serve. Always pursue to increase your domain expertise no matter what!

On an individual basis, what can you do to improve your domain expertise? We know of one particular CSM that made it a point to attend all of her customers' annual conferences. It was a simple tactic but astute. Attending industry conferences serves three purposes.

- It helps you learn about the trends in the industry or category.
- It helps you understand how your customers deal with those trends.
- You network with individuals in the same industry or category, opening doors for more in-depth learning and possible mentor relationships.

Network with Mentors and Industry Experts

Finding a mentor can be life-changing. Mentors can take many forms, like a family friend, a seasoned colleague, or someone you met at a networking event. Ideally, you should find a mentor active in the industry you are trying to learn more about. Such an individual is able to provide the most up-to-date developments as well as share the day-to-day realities of the industry. Once you do connect with an industry mentor, ask deeper level questions like "What do you think are the biggest challenges facing this industry?" or "What are the big technological disruptions?" Also, make sure you put yourself out there. If there's a local event with a panel discussion or expert talk, this could be particularly beneficial to you. Treat it like a university lecture; be attentive, ask questions, and take notes.

When we considered adding a different perspective on this topic, we immediately turned to Chrisy Woll. Chrisy is the Vice President of Customer Success at CampusLogic, a student financial success platform that simplifies the student journey, driving access, informed borrowing, and completion. She understands the need for quality education and mentoring for up and coming CSMs. Chrisy shared her story of learning from one of her mentors and the importance of investing in learning about your industry to become the best in the business.

How Do You Build an Expert? By Stalking.

By Chrisy Woll, Vice President of Customer Success at CampusLogic

The advice was simple: stalk rock stars for at least five hours a week. Ok, fine. That's not exactly how he said it. "He" was the CEO of a fast-growing SaaS company. I was an individual contributor new to everything: the company, our industry, SaaS, and definitely stalking. We were a small start-up focused on being nimble – and definitely in charge of owning our own growth. Sound familiar?

What he actually said: "If you want to be successful here, you'll need to spend an extra five hours a week outside of work hours learning about our industry." My strategy was simple because I'm good at simple. Find the smartest person in the room, on the team, in the industry, and stalk them. Not in an overly creepy kind of way. More in an *"always watching what they do, where they find their information, and what they say"* kind of way.

(continued)

(continued)

There were three things I learned from my "rock stars."

Rock Stars Are Voracious Content Consumers. Books, blogs, websites, tweets, rants, essays, newsletters – rock stars consume *All. The. Things.* from influencers in their industry. Do the same. Find influencers (your rock stars will point you to them) and follow them on social media, subscribe to their YouTube channels, bookmark their podcasts. PS: make sure you consume the content, otherwise don't bother stalking.

Imitation is the Sincerest Form of Flattery. There's nothing wrong with being a copycat until you've had time to develop a well-informed opinion to yourself. Listen to the rock stars on the team (because you're stalking them already) and repeat the things they say. One BIG caveat: don't say things you can't live up to. Example: a rock star I worked with/stalked often said, "It all comes down to the brass tacks." I'm sure in the right context that expression creates a lot of urgency about whatever the heck brass tacks mean. However, if I tried to pull that off, it would be a tragic mess! So, copy what people say but put your flavor and personality into it.

Rock Stars Wear Their Customers' Shoes. By far, this is the most important thing. It is also why I saved it for last. Rock stars care deeply about the customer. They learn about what customers care about. They put themselves in their shoes, think about their day-to-day life, pain points, goals, and dreams. And they think about how they can help with all of it. Master this skill, and you'll connect on a human level. That is **more** important than being the biggest expert in any room.

Having a mentor is as important as having professional goals. Mentors can draw advice and guidance from a wellspring of their vast field knowledge, product expertise, and best practice methods. They can also help you traverse the company waters. Find one or find a select few that you can turn to when you need them most. Also, consider seeking mentors that are not in your field. Remember, Customer Success is a company-wide endeavor, and mentoring is a part of that great work.

Aside from mentors, you should actively follow and participate in a variety of online industry and category community discussion groups. LinkedIn, for example, is a great place to find lively and relevant discussions of current trends in practically any industry and category.

Pro tips:
- Narrow your choices, favor groups with larger memberships or groups that are more local.
- Don't be afraid to post questions and ask for advice on topics relevant to that industry.
- Follow influential companies in the industry.
- Follow industry bloggers.

Go old-school: read books, subscribe to printed magazines or specialty industry newsletters. Find ones that appeal to you. WebWire[1] has a list of a wide range of trade publications by industry and category. Look for industry digital news sources. Leverage Google News alerts. Whatever it is, remember, your goal is to be the best Customer Success Manager for your customers and for the industry you and they serve.

Product Expertise Is Your Ticket to Greatness

When it comes to appraising CSMs, product expertise differentiates the best ones from the rest. Having an intimate knowledge of your product is a skill that will help you unlock value very quickly for your customers and build trust with them. Frankly, it's not optional if you want to rise to the top of your team and be the best CSM possible. We've encountered far too many CS professionals that believe success can be delivered to their customers strictly based on their industry experience or their ability to build empathetic relationships. While these skills are absolutely relevant and valuable, the most successful CSMs have deep product expertise in their repertoire. Consider this: your customers are paying for your product, not your affable interactions. They expect interactions with representatives from your company that can draw further value from their investment with your company and its product. The expectation of product expertise is even higher with their assigned CSM – you!

Of course, the amount of product knowledge required depends on the role description of CSMs at your company. At the very least, CSMs need to articulate the benefits of your product, and how they are differentiated versus your competitors. In some companies, CSMs are expected to technically assess the configuration and deployment of your product at a customer and provide a point of view on whether it adheres to best practices.

Here are a few strategies to increase your product knowledge:

1. **Leverage available literature.**
   If you search, you will probably find plenty of rich content already available within your company. Look for product or demo videos. Most companies have these available for their customers, so leverage the same material. If there is any virtual or onsite training available for your customers, ask to join the class. Ask your Product team to share the same materials they use to onboard their own new staff. Many companies have excellent "best practice" articles available on their support or customer community websites. Also, track down customer success stories and case studies from your Marketing team or recent conferences and trade shows. Review them to know how customers get value from your product.

2. **Learn from your colleagues.**
   Make friends with teammates in Solutions Consulting or Sales Engineering. They are the pre-sales technical teammates who work with the Sales Reps and prospective customers during the sales cycle. They are adept at talking about the benefits of your product, its competitive advantages, and can demonstrate the most relevant features of the product. Try joining in on some of their sales demonstrations. It gives a proper perspective on how they position and "pitch" the product and the types of questions your prospective customers might have. This vantage point gives you a first-hand perspective on what problems customers are trying to solve with your product. Don't stop there. Consider spending some time with your technical support team until you have an appropriate level of product mastery. This experience is an excellent way to learn the frequently asked questions about the product. It's also a suitable manner in which to acquaint yourself with go-to resources on the Support team that you'll occasionally need to lean on in your day to day as a CSM. The same approach should be applied to your product teams. Some innovative companies have a resource-sharing model where every Product Manager spends a couple of weeks with customer-facing teams. This time helps develop more empathy for customer situations.

3. **Practice the sales demo and pitch.**

   You will be asked often, as a CSM, to walk through a demonstration of your product with new customer stakeholders. It could even be to an entire group of new users. Sometimes this will happen literally on-demand and unexpectedly. You must be able and ready to articulate the product's value and purpose, and demonstrate its functionality with as much, if not more, precision as your best salesperson. It is advisable to actually practice demoing in front of a real group of people, such as your own CS team.

4. **User group meet-ups.**

   Many companies host regular user group meetings intended for their customers. It is generally a forum to network and share ideas and innovative ways of using your company's product. These meet-ups often afford you a unique opportunity to hear from a diverse set of companies, the various challenges they face, how they are using your company's products to solve real problems, and creative use-cases.

A big part of a CSM's job is to improve the product continually by being the voice of the customer to your own Product team. Customers will use your product in a myriad of ways. Eventually, they will encounter what appears to be a product-gap or shortcoming of functionality. Customers will then request product enhancements and often do so with a sense of urgency. In that situation, you must have a high level of product proficiency to even recognize if the request is something that can already be solved by the product in its current form. In other words, if you don't know the product very well, how can you know if it will or will not solve the customer's unique situation?

Even if you know with certainty that the product can't handle their particular use-case perfectly, your first reaction still shouldn't be "We need to put in an enhancement request." Instead, your first reaction should be to exhaust the current capabilities of your product, putting your creative hat on, asking your peers about the customer use-case, and brainstorming a dozen different workarounds, all with the goal of solving the customer's problem. Enhancement requests should really be a last-resort option. Again, this all assumes you have a high-level of product competency to even discern the difference.

Please recall the Consumption Gap diagram (Figure 2.2) that we covered in Chapter 2. Your job as a CSM is to maximize the use of the product **in its current state!** Yes, you are expected to raise new and valuable inputs that help improve your product over time, but you have an obligation to filter through all of the noise and only surface to your Product team the most valuable and impactful product improvements represented across your customer base. Taking this approach, you will have a higher success rate in persuading Product and Engineering to listen to your needs, especially if they have confidence in your product expertise. It gives you far more credibility both internally and with your customers.

•••

In this chapter, hopefully, you picked up some tactical tips for developing industry, category, and product mastery and understand how they are critical to your success as a Customer Success Manager. Take these new insights as you progress to the next chapter where you'll gain practical advice on how to empathize and build relationships with customers. Combined with learning how to become a problem-solving consultant to your customers covered in Chapter 6, you will be on your way to Customer Success Management greatness.

Endnote

1. Retrieved from: https://www.webwire.com/IndustryList.asp.

5

Learn How to Empathize and Build Relationships with Customers

Of all the skills that a Customer Success Manager should master, the ability to empathize and build relationships with customers is of the utmost importance. It needs to be approached with a simple perspective in mind. Your customer is your customer because, at some point, an executive on their side decided to engage your company. You are in what is essentially an on-demand relationship; one that you've been thrust into. As a CSM, you are at the center of that business relationship. You need to quickly move it from the formal business arrangement, which can be a bit awkward at the beginning, to a far more human-centric and trust-based partnership. Getting to that state rapidly is vital in order to create a foundation of success with your customers.

To give you a different flavor on this "soft-skills" topic, we have distilled the critical skill of building empathetic relationships with customers down to these Seven Principles:

1. Be introspective and self-aware.
2. Communicate with intent, precision, and persuasion and become a trusted advisor.

61

3. Consistently follow-up to create and grow trust.
4. How to respond when you don't know the answer.
5. Stay focused and positive when situations are difficult and learn from them.
6. Engage people in-depth and with a #humanfirst lens of compassion.
7. Genuinely connect with customers because it is personal, and it is your business.

While some of these topics are certainly not new or unique, Customer Success is a new profession that demands different business motions and requires a more human-centric focus. In line with that approach, we are incredibly fortunate to work at a company that has genuinely put a concerted effort into defining, practicing, and living out a stated set of core values. We believe these values and stated purpose translate and apply to the Customer Success profession in general. Not only do they serve as our North Star, we sincerely believe they should be considered the **ethical standards of behavior for all Customer Success Managers.**

Anthony Kennada masterfully described the advent of Gainsight's core values and purpose in his book *Category Creation: How to Build a Brand that Customers, Employees, and Investors Will Love.*[1] He stated, "From the early days of the company, we knew that we wanted to build a company that behaved in accordance with the following principles:

- **The Golden Rule:** Treat people the way you'd like to be treated.
- **Success for All:** Our 'bottom line' requires us to drive success for not only shareholders, but also customers, teammates, their families, and our communities around us.
- **Childlike Joy:** Bring the kid in you to work every day.
- **Shoshin:** Cultivate a 'Beginner's Mind.'
- **Stay Thirsty, My Friends:** Have ambition that comes from within."

However, the core values weren't enough. Anthony goes on to affirm "We decided on the WHY that would keep us going long beyond the day-to-day. Our purpose at Gainsight is: **To be living proof that you can win in business while being human-first.** Human-first means always thinking about people in the decisions you make about business."

Now let's take a look at the seven principles of building relationships with customers.

1. Be Introspective and Self-Aware

In order to be human-first, you have to be fully aware of the first human you encounter every single moment of existence: which is YOU. One of the most essential characteristics of a great CSM is being self-aware. We all come with our own stories and backgrounds. There are indeed things we have learned and experienced that add value to what we have to say and give. Sometimes they are not so good and appear as idiosyncrasies, peccadilloes, or even baggage. Your story (the good, the bad, and the ugly) will impact how you approach your customers.

Before you try to solve your customer's challenges, you should take the time to consider your own biases. For example, if your stress levels or anxieties are running particularly high, that energy will undoubtedly transfer to your business situation and customer. As much as we think we can engage with minimum emotion while doing our business-jobs, the simple fact is we are human, and our emotions and behaviors are perceivable and can be contagious. Before you approach your customer to establish and grow a genuine relationship, acknowledge your stress levels so you can have a better chance at controlling them in a better way for you, your company, and especially your customers. Be genuine about your fears and anxieties and do your best to "let it go."

In the same manner that you examine your fears, be candid to yourself about your goals and hopes for success. These can be positive incentives that inspire your customer relationships. The author Susan Sontag once said, "Courage is as contagious as fear." Ponder that for a moment. If you give an effort to being genuinely curious, humble, respectful to fellow human beings, and show a desire to partner with your customers for their success, your mental status will default to be positive. Make that your core and operate from it. There is an honesty to your emotions that will reflect in your behavior. They are not techniques to be adopted. They must be real.

While it may be easy to dismiss all of this as non-business fluff, the best CSMs are very self-aware and emotionally connected to the people they serve. Yes! Emotionally connected. This profession is very much a human endeavor, requiring mastery in human engagement. This applies even to the tech-touch CSM that never speaks to a customer directly. In fact, they have to approach their work with an even greater focus and consideration to the real people at the other end of their automation engagements.

You must also be aware of not overextending confidences so that it breaches into hubris. Authentic confidence is found in humility. It's a careful balance to maintain for sure, especially since you must "own the room," "be the expert," and "drive your customer." To many, humility implies weakness. It is ironic that the word humility has its roots in Middle English and Latin, and it means "of the earth" or "not far from the ground."

True humility means you are grounded. You can relate to others that are "of the earth." It means you are human. Being humble means you know to assert yourself in a **positive** way that enables others to follow your leadership. Humility also means that you know that you are not full of yourself. There is room for more knowledge, and there is more to learn. Continually learning and improving is the mark of a great CSM.

The Customer Success Manager Credo

One of the best exercises that Dan Steinman, Gainsight's first Chief Customer Officer, required as part of the vetting process of hiring new CSMs in the early days of Gainsight was to have candidates create and deliver a personal "Customer Success Manager creed." It was intended to be a short one-page personal proclamation of how you would carry out your duties as a CSM at Gainsight. Dan gave no further instructions. The assignment was brilliant! It forced the candidate to come up with something original and personal; something substantive that would resonate for Gainsight, executive management, peers, and customers. Over the years, we've shared this tactic with a number of customers. They too adopted a similar practice and some even required it of their existing CSMs as part of an off-site team-building activity. It is a timeless exercise. Figure 5.1 shows an example of an actual Customer Success Manager creed that was submitted by a Gainsight candidate (now an author of this book):

Be Joyous, It's Contagious
Have fun, laugh, laugh-a-lot, love your work, let your passion show.
Evolve You
Be a better version of YOU than you were a few breaths ago.

Do Right/Be Kind
Have a superhero desire for doing the right thing but do so with humility and kindness.

Be Dependable
Honor your commitments; do things NOW!

All Things Are Possible
Move through life as though it is impossible to fail; we have your back!

Be the Expert
Be the expert in the room about our products & methodologies.

Improve Your Product
Be the #1 advocate for product improvement to our product team.

Listen & Learn
Be permanently poised to listen and learn from our customers.

Establish Value
Build customer loyalty by providing value & meaningful solutions that evolve with their changing needs.

Know Your Customer
Know your stakeholders well; make sure our Product Value is aligned with their success.

Create Stickiness
Every customer engagement is an opportunity to create additional product/ brand loyalty.

Celebrate Success in a Big Way
Retentions & upsells are the lifeblood: celebrate and proclaim successes!

Wear Many Hats, With Confidence
Do whatever it takes to get the job done; kick ass and do everything with confidence.

Step Out-of-the-Whirlwind
Every day, tackle at least one goal outside of your whirlwind.

Figure 5.1   A personal Customer Success creed.

Assess each of the commitments through your own personal lens. What would yours look like? What personal truisms would you include? How do you perceive yourself and how do you want others to experience you? If you want to be a great CSM, you have to be introspective and self-aware. Doing so will establish a solid foundation for you as a CS professional to better serve your customers.

2. Communicate with Intent, Precision, and Persuasion: Be a Trusted Advisor

The term *trusted advisor* is so overused that the meaning has been diluted. In fact, you probably can't find a consistent definition. Let's turn then to David Maister and Charles Green, authors of *The Trusted Advisor,* for their affirmative attempt at standardizing the phrase. A trusted advisor, according to Maister and Green, "is the person the client turns to when an issue first arises, often in times of great urgency: a crisis, a change, a triumph, or a defeat."[2]

Now ask yourself, will your customer urgently reach out to you when there is a crisis, a change, or a win, or a loss? For many, the answer should be an immediate "yes," in particular if it's in the context of your product. However, ask the question from a broader perspective. Does your customer urgently reach out when they have a strategic business-level crisis, a company-wide change, a huge success, or massive company failure *unrelated* to your product? The answer will likely be a "no." As a CSM, however, you absolutely want to forge a deep trust relationship so you can answer in the affirmative.

Being considered a true trusted advisor means that you understand the customer's business with a level of intimacy that goes beyond the purview of your engagement. You understand the roles and various influences of the people you interact with and how *they* are measured by *their* organization. It means you understand *their* objectives, *their* goals, and *their* pain points. It means you clearly know *their* definition of *their* success and more importantly how you can help *them* achieve it. This level of intimate understanding demonstrates that you care about *their* business first. It also shows that your product complements and is at-service to *their* goals, not just to your company objectives.

So how do you attain the status of becoming a true trusted advisor? Start by communicating with intent, precision, and persuasion.

Intent

While there are many forms of communication and engagement with your customers, there are two specifically that must cease immediately. Repeat after me: **"ALL STATUS AND CHECK-IN CALLS MUST DIE."** Most of these types of calls are a waste of time. For far too many companies, they have devolved into a cadence of information dumps and forced functions to ensure you and your customers are meeting regularly. In the same light, you must never again place a call or send an email to a customer simply to see how they're doing or to get a sentiment from them. If you are doing either of these today, stop it now!

You are a CS professional and your primary charter is to drive your customer to their measured success. Simply checking-in on them with no other purpose does not drive value. They don't need a best friend that is calling just to see how things are going. While that may seem like the "kind" act to do, you are literally wasting your and the customer's time. Their company has engaged your company to help drive toward a business goal. As a CSM, it is precisely your job to know how the customer is doing without having to ask them. It is truly the antithesis of what CS is all about. When you communicate with your customers, check your intent. Be sure your message maps back to their success goals and how your company's product will help attain them.

Precision

Precision and purpose are even more important when engaging an executive or C-level. Be brief and be clear on your ask of them. Leverage their role, presence, and influence. In other words, don't have the executive along for the ride. Don't have meetings to only touch base or update your customer. Quickly demonstrate how their engagement with you has moved them closer to their goals and added value. Most importantly, when you have a captive audience, which includes emails, always have in your minds-eye what action you are attempting to solicit from them and how it will bring them closer to their desired goals.

Persuasion

The last component of establishing a trust relationship is communicating with persuasion. As a CSM, you must master the art of persuasion. Practically every communication you have with a customer is about persuading them to do something different than they were doing before. It is all for the pursuit of their stated objectives. Your task is to convince them to follow your advice, use your product, and make operational changes.

3. Consistently Follow-Up to Create and Grow Trust

One of the most important traits of a CSM is to have consistent follow-up. It outwardly demonstrates to your customers and your coworkers that they matter and are worth your time. Do you send an email almost immediately following every customer engagement? Consider this angle: you should want to be better than all the other CSMs from different vendors that your customer engages on a regular basis. You want to be the CSM that always follows up immediately after a call or meeting and the one with a reputation of remarkable consistency.

At Gainsight, we have a very aspirational yet very serious policy of responding to emails or internal messages within 24 hours. It's woven into our company culture. It's aspirational because it is REALLY hard to adhere to that kind of timeline when your inbox can be fed with over 250 new emails a day. It's serious because we do our best to hold each other accountable when we don't respond in that timeframe. The overall result, we hope, is a culture of hyper-responsiveness to one another, to our customers, partners, and prospects.

Customer Success Managers don't have the luxury of playing email-victim. As much as everyone at Gainsight would love to always meet the 24-hour rule, the truth is we don't hit it 100% of the time, and we feel terrible. Personally, it doesn't make you feel good because you know there is a person on the other end waiting for your response or acknowledgment. As a CSM, you must master the skill of follow-up. Are you a master yet of your inbox? If you are, please share your secret sauce with the rest of the world. If not, it's time to try a different tactic because no matter your disposition on this topic, customers in the digital economy expect an ever more rapid and consistent follow-up.

4. How to Respond When You Don't Know the Answer

There's an old adage, "fake it until you make it." While this approach can be applied in many customer situations, you would be best to not employ it as a CSM. So how do you respond when you legitimately don't know the answer?

Ultimately, it is a question of trust. Humans are very good at deciphering the truth. We've spent a lifetime practicing. If you are ever in a situation when you're not very confident of an answer, your best approach is to not make something up or dance-around a possible response. Your customer, a human on the receiving end, will perceive even the slightest fault in your tone or message. Rather, be fully transparent and don't use phrases that raise uncertainty like "I'm not sure." Rather, follow these guidelines to ensure you don't lose your customer's trust in situations when you don't have an answer:

- BE DIRECT: it's okay to state that you don't know the answer to a question. However, you must provide a follow-up commitment target in hours or days.
- STATE WHAT YOU KNOW: while you may not know the full or conclusive answer, it's likely that you know or have information that is pertinent. State what you do know to the customer in the context of your discovery. It will affirm your understanding of the question and will convey that the forthcoming answer will have more precision.
- COMPLIMENT: compliment the customer on how great a question it is but don't be patronizing. Be sincere, especially if it's a question you haven't heard prior. Again, provide a follow-up commitment target in hours or days.

- PAUSE: pause and think before responding. It demonstrates contemplation and steadiness on your part; that you are considering all of the known options before just blurting out that you don't know.
- NOTE THE STEPS YOU'LL TAKE: be sure to convey to the customer the various steps and persons you need to speak to, as well as the timeframe required to derive an answer.

Whatever you do, don't be apologetic for not knowing an answer. You have to be as confident in stating that you don't know an answer as when you do know the answer. You are, after all, human. Customers are too, so they get the occasional gaps in knowledge. In order to maintain and grow your customer's trust in you, be sincere in your response and follow-up in the timeframe you provided.

5. Stay Focused and Positive When Situations Are Difficult; Learn From Them

In the world of customer success, there will be many ups and downs literally throughout your day. You could be on a call in the morning and have the absolute best engagement ever with the largest customer in your book of business. Then, the very next call could be your most loyal customer telling you the news that they will not be renewing their annual subscription with you, despite all of the history and recent efforts to meet their changing needs.

Staying positive no matter what hits you requires a grittiness and a spirit of determination that is steadfast. The CS profession requires an almost fundamental disposition of positivity. Almost like a salesperson. They are driven by an optimistic belief that every lead is a potential close-win deal. Similarly, CSMs should be driven by an optimistic belief that every customer within their purview has the potential to succeed, resulting in advocacy, renewal, and expansion.

You are constantly pulled in a thousand different directions and you must consistently display a fortitude to do what is right for the customer, right for your shareholders, and what is right for you. For example, while you may be committed to ensuring your customers and your shareholders attain their goals, you can't sacrifice your own personal health if it means working 80 hours a week all the time. That's just not sustainable. You have to stay true to your mission of ensuring that the customer is attaining their desired outcomes while considering your company goals and your own work-life balance.

Being a CSM can be an amazingly rewarding experience, but it can also be exhausting. Some days you feel like you're never winning. All your customers might be complaining about something or you may feel like you're not able to give all of them the attention that's needed. You will have wins and those will be awesome! The Customer Success Manager literally can be the difference between a customer renewing and expanding versus churning and cancelling their contract. It's about finding the balance and inner strength to stay in the game because great CSMs foster great customers.

At some point along your journey as a CSM, you'll cross a threshold where you'll say to yourself, and maybe even to your boss, "BRING IT ON! I can take on any account. There isn't a customer situation that I can't handle. I am the super-Customer Success Manager and I can conquer the world!"

6. Read People In-Depth and With a #HumanFirst Lens of Compassion

Everyone has a story. They have unique backgrounds, histories, challenges, struggles, achievements, and everything in between. Your customers are people. The best CSMs spend as much time learning about the individuals at their customers as their customers' businesses. Ask questions to learn about your customers' backgrounds, experiences, and why they have come to believe what they do. Engage them genuinely to learn more about them.

Reading people is understanding them through a lens of compassion, and it requires "insight." Most definitions center on the word "intuitive" and how it leads you to a deeper understanding of a person, a thing, or a situation. Intuition is the "ah-ha" moment when there is an instantaneous or quickening of understanding. It goes beyond knowing the facts or following a scripted playbook. It is the consumption and processing of all the inputs about your customer at any given time. Yes, that includes dashboards and Health Scores. It also consists of conversations, listening to the tone of their voice during a call or their phrasing and choice of words in an email, and looking into the eyes of your client. Sometimes it is perceiving that there is something wrong when an otherwise happy and healthy customer becomes unresponsive all of a sudden. Logic may suggest "Everything is fine. Their recent NPS score is great." You may even find yourself reflecting "I spoke with them last week. Why should I investigate?" You dismiss the "gut feeling" because all the practical information refutes it. Yet, there is still this urge from within that something is wrong. That urge, prompt, or gut feeling is a type of insight that you should follow.

The security expert, Gavin de Becker, wrote at length about insight and intuition in his book *The Gift of Fear*. He believes that what many people attribute to an almost supernatural state is fundamental to every human being. This "gift" is higher than logic and is very much a part of the cognitive. De Becker stated, "Intuition is the journey from A to Z without stopping at any other letter along the way. It is knowing without knowing why."[3]

If insight and intuition is a "knowing," how do you use it as a CSM? If a customer calls and is unpleasant, maybe even yelling at you, you might later find out it had nothing to do with you, your product, or the customer's experience but rather something stressful in their personal or work life. Yet, you somehow knew. You allowed yourself to handle the situation with compassion instead of jumping immediately to conclusions or firing back at your customer. It is a very human process and you have permission to be human. In fact, you are encouraged as a CSM to lean into the human trait of intuition and insight, even with all the data, telemetry, technology, and automation. Customer Success Management at its core is a human endeavor.

Knowing how to discern the best path forward in any situation is an elemental trait of great CSMs. In business, it is rarely about making a good or bad decision, a legal or illegal one, or even moral or ethical one. It's really about deciding which path is good, better, or best for all your stakeholders. If you have a heart with great intention to do what is best for your customer and you believe you have the customer's success in mind while also considering your company's objectives, you almost can't lose. Sure, there will be occasions of failures or shortcomings but those are rarely intentional. When you leverage your natural human insight along with all the other data-inputs and can respond with recommended paths forward, your customer relationships will blossom.

7. Genuinely Connect with Customers: it is Personal and it is Your Business

As a CSM, you have an imperative to honor the relationship you were handed. Think about all of the money, time, effort, and energy spent on getting and sustaining the customer to this point. It is now in your hands to foster and grow. For far too long, businesses have conditioned their employees, and entire generations, with the mindset that business is business and not personal. One of the reasons the customer success profession is thriving is because it has changed that distorted approach to engaging customers. It is personal, and it is your business! This is the long-haul relationship we are after and there is an intimacy that should be attained with your customer. Of course, we are not alone in this belief.

Mary Poppen, Chief Customer Officer at Glint, believes in the need for a shift in business processes and mindsets to be more empathetic, both for the customer and the employee. Ultimately, she wants to see the customer become the hero – something that she believes is only possible through intimate customer relationships. Although Mary has over 20 years of business consulting and executive experience and holds a master's degree in industrial/organizational psychology, it was a sincere passion for this subject that drew us to her.

Customer Intimacy is the Key to Genuine Connection and Lifelong Partnerships

By Mary Poppen, *Chief Customer Officer at Glint*

As you should know by now, a CSM is responsible for the overall success of their customers. They have the most significant ability to foster intimacy in the customer relationship. While some people will shy away from the word "intimacy," there is not another term that captures the

(continued)

(continued)

completeness of the relationship. A CSM needs to know the customer so well that they anticipate their needs before they happen. Once you shift your mindset in this way, you are no longer a guide to your customers. You are a partner on their journey with the ability to have a positive impact on their lives.

When interviewing potential Customer Success Managers or reviewing current CSM's skills to align them with our customer-centric strategy, I look for the three essential skills of curiosity, a focus on results, and empathy to ensure they will be successful in creating an incredible customer experience. Together these abilities can create a long-lasting customer partnership. Let us begin with what I believe each of those skills means.

> **Curiosity** for a CSM is to look for all the possibilities in every situation. It is both the "why" and the "why not." Through the lens of curiosity, you understand problems and how best to resolve them. In asking "why" you are looking to choose the optimal resolution in every circumstance. By asking "why not" you show your ability to be open-minded to consider the advice and outside options from alternate sources. Curiosity is also continuously learning, searching to understand new perspectives. By being perpetually curious, you will improve and continue to evolve your customer relationships.
>
> **Focus on results** is often characterized as solving the problem in the fastest manner possible. Truly focusing on results means the completion of the task where all the needs are met, both for your business and your customers. The best solutions are not always the obvious ones. You must seek to resolve every situation optimally. Focusing on results is also taking accountability and having integrity. When you focus on results you acknowledge issues, take responsibility, and always follow through.
>
> **Empathy** has become a word that is often used, but it seems it is rarely understood. Empathy is not merely trying to understand another person's plight. It is putting yourself in the other person's place. You must know who they are and where they are coming from – completely. Empathy allows you to respond in a way that is genuine, caring, and on target. Cultivating empathy starts with

listening intently to your customers and understanding what they are telling you. When you holistically hear them, you can respond to their specific needs, concerns, or questions by bringing in the right resources at the right time in the right way. Ultimately, you create a strong partnership that is difficult for any competitor to match.

As stated earlier, a CSM is responsible for the overall success of their customers. They have an exceptional ability to foster customer intimacy because of their position. I have used this term *customer intimacy* for years to describe the pinnacle relationship where the CSM knows the customer better than anyone else. As a CSM, you understand through an empathetic mindset what the customer needs, when they need it, and how to deliver it. You ultimately know what the customer needs before they do! This level of partnership makes it far less likely that your customer will consider a competitor. It also ensures that you are viewed as a trusted advisor rather than merely a vendor. You have become the partner on the customer's journey. Empathy, curiosity, and a focus on results are three differentiating keys to CSM success and the secret sauce in building high-performing CS teams.

●●●

The ability to build relationships with customers is the highest virtue of your role as a CSM. Sure, there is a business imperative to customer success that drives revenue and we will certainly progress into the business tactics in the subsequent chapters. Your mindset and focus as a CSM, however, has to shift from you or your company to that of your customers. Moreover, your customers, at the core, are people who want to succeed just like you do in their jobs and in their lives. How awesome is it to be in a role, as a Customer Success Manager, where you are encouraged to advocate for someone else's success?

The Seven Principles covered herein hopefully have given you some additional skills and ideas for introspection. Putting them into action will allow for a more human-centric focus in your day-to-day efforts as a Customer Success Manager.

Endnotes

1. Kenneda, A. (2019). *Category Creation: How to Build a Brand that Customers, Employees, and Investors Will Love*. Hoboken, NJ: John Wiley & Sons, Inc.
2. Maister, D. and Green, C. (2000). *The Trusted Advisor*. New York, NY: The Free Press.
3. De Becker, G. (1997). *The Gift of Fear*. New York, NY: Little, Brown, and Company.

PART III

Operationalizing Customer Success

6

Preparing for Your Engagements and Asking Questions Like a Problem-Solving Consultant

In most companies, data is spread across multiple places. There are ticketing or support case systems. Some companies rely on product usage and telemetry tools. They also have offline documents, and don't be surprised if you find sticky notes at people's desks! There is also the almighty Customer Relationship Management (CRM) system which is excellent for storing data but notoriously difficult for finding it. Every team or function, from Customer Success, Sales, and Marketing has access to at least a few of these data stores that are tied to their critical day-to-day operations. The disparity in data storage, access, and usage means everyone in the company has a different understanding of the customer depending on what data they have access to. Worse still, no one has a comprehensive understanding of the customer. This disparity is detrimental to the health of the customer and your relationship with them.

In an article from the *Harvard Business Review* entitled "Unlock the mysteries of your customer relationships," the authors Jill Avery, Susan Fournier, and John Wittenbraker reported on data sharing.[1] Their research showed many companies could increase their understanding of their customers by boosting the relational intelligence simply by utilizing data across the organization. Many companies "receive vast amounts of data – via e-mails, online chat sessions between customers and reps, and phone calls – that contain relational signals, but they're poor at *collecting* and *analyzing* all this information." They concluded that just by participating in data gathering techniques, such as surveys, the customers were giving signals that conveyed "what kinds of relationships customers want." The key was to start "listening for and capturing them." Despite this knowledge, companies were not only underutilizing the information gathered, but they also weren't storing it or sharing it advantageously.

The authors were not alone in affirming the correlation between leveraging data from multiple sources across an organization to improve customer insights. The importance of data usage and sharing was the topic of a 2018 MIT Sloan Management Review report entitled "Using Analytics to Improve Customer Engagement." The authors, Sam Ransbotham and David Kiron, found a disparity between data collection and proper use or application. Their research "finds that innovative, analytically mature organizations make use of data from multiple sources: customers, vendors, regulators, and even competitors."[2]

The Need for a 360° View of the Customer

What are the typical symptoms of not having a comprehensive understanding of the customer? It will be hard for your teams to collaborate on a customer. It will take more time to prepare for customer interactions. Your employees will have inconsistent or even conflicting information about a customer. Different systems often contradict each other on the facts of a customer. Worst of all, information kept in notes in a non-centralized place becomes unshared and often inaccessible. Data is not institutionalized. Instead, it exists in various isolated compartments, including people's brains. Data is often out of sight of teams that could desperately use the additional details. Further, lack of data consistency makes things disorganized, and the information tends to disappear when an employee transfers off a customer.

When information gathering and storage is done right, a company can aggregate critical customer data into a single source to provide a holistic view that enables the entire organization to do better work. To get there, you need to be able to capture vital information across the organizational teams easily (e.g. Sales, Success, Support, Services) and the types of data (e.g. product usage, interactions). Every team needs up-to-date insights into relevant business relationships, products, and service engagements. The "Best in Class" companies practice this process. It enables them to share their ideas directly with customers, which promotes transparency and collaboration in mutually delivering customer success.

Where the Data Comes From

If you are using a Customer Success platform, the value of that platform quickly multiplies if you can aggregate these sources of data into the platform. In our experience, the most impactful five sources of data include product usage/telemetry data, support ticket information (includes reported bugs), training and certification completed by your users, surveys (such as Net Promoter Score, Customer Satisfaction, Customer Effort Score), and the status of any ongoing professional services engagements. In large enterprises, these would need to be collected, sorted, and presented in your Customer Success platform, by-products, and business units to be useful.

If you don't have access to any of these sources of information, don't despair. There is much you can do to help your customers while you wait for this data. There's a treasure trove of information residing in all the calls and meetings different people in your company are having with your customers. Make it possible and easy for everyone to capture their notes after their customer interactions (Figure 6.1). Make it easy to share and collaborate. For example, have the ability to at-mention people and comment on notes. It will go a long way in fostering collaboration. It is also essential to capture a few other metadata from your calls and meetings:

- Who from the customer attended?
- Who from your company attended?
- When did the interaction happen?
- How long did it last?

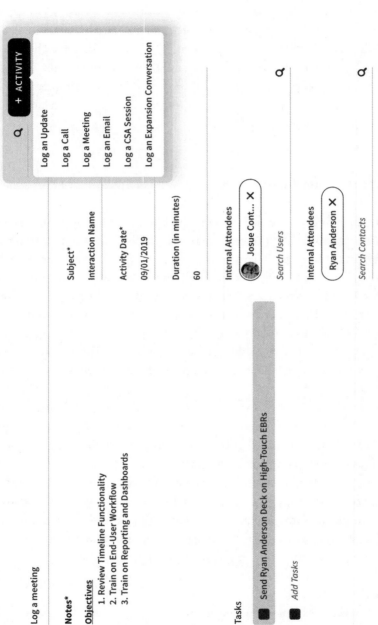

Figure 6.1 Example template to take notes from your calls or meetings.

- What was the sentiment on the call? How is it trending vs. the previous interaction?
- What type of interaction format was it? For example, call, meeting, email, internal update, etc.
- Bonus: What was the desired outcome from the interaction? For example, executive sponsorship, advocacy, expansion/sales, etc.
- Bonus: What are the follow-up actions from the interaction?
- Bonus: What documents/attachments were used in the interaction?

Now that you have all of these data and insights in one place, make sure you reference those before a call or meeting. Some CSMs even pull up the product usage or call notes "live" in a meeting to show how they are actively partnering with the customer in their success. It is an activity that is very convincing. No matter how you proceed, remember that it is preparation and due diligence that will make a difference in your customer-facing interactions.

Do Your Homework: Prepare for Every Customer Engagement

Putting all the skills and competencies required to be a great Customer Success Manager into practice is not easy. It's incredibly challenging to perform all of the necessary functions of a CSM while keeping everything within your purview. However, there is one skill that rises to the top in this ambitious profession: *preparation*. When contemplating a contributor for this topic, one of the very first people we considered was our colleague, Elaine Cleary. She is a true virtuoso of the craft and has dedicated her career to delighting customers while delivering business outcomes. At Gainsight, we once preserved the title of Principal Customer Success Manager for those very select, rare individuals that achieve and perform at the highest attainable levels of effectiveness and mastery of the CS profession. To date, no one has been granted this unique designation, besides Elaine. She is a CS superstar and a true role model of an ideal customer success practitioner. We are truly honored to have her share some thoughts and advice on the importance of preparation.

Prepare for Every Customer Engagement

By Elaine Cleary, Principal Customer Success Manager, Director of Education Services at Gainsight

In the fast-paced world of Customer Success, being proactive and prepared can often be overlooked and overshadowed with the demands of putting out customer fires. One of the best ways to shift the pendulum from being reactive to proactive is to consider specific strategies for how to prepare for different types of customer engagements. Doing so helps you maximize the value of those interactions. The key is to stick to your plan, no matter how busy you are. Don't work harder; work smarter!

Let's begin with some basics. Every customer engagement should have a clear *purpose* and attainable *expectations* on the desired outcome. You must also know your *audience* and adjust your approach appropriately. In addition, both you and your customers have objectives and goals in mind for each engagement. It's important to recognize that your respective goals are not likely to be the same. How well you navigate the who, what, and why makes a big difference to your long-term mutual success.

Before you prepare, here are some important considerations:

Considerations	Examples	Tips
Basic engagements	■ Face-to-face meetings ■ Phone/web calls ■ Emails	■ Choose the right engagement type for your message and audience ■ For meetings and calls, begin and end on time if not early ■ Everyone is busy, so get to the point quickly and take good notes ■ For on-site meetings, confirm address/building access. Don't forget the firm handshake and good eye contact – it matters!

Considerations	Examples	Tips
Goal or desired outcome – yours and theirs!	▪ Share information ▪ Improve value of partnership ▪ Communicate a call to action ▪ Simple request like a reference or knowledge transfer on best practice ▪ More complex request like speaking engagement, renewal, or upsell conversation	▪ Be prepared to state your goal up front and get acknowledgment ▪ Clarify their goal ▪ Table or put in a "parking lot" any discussions that stray from the primary objective
Typical expected audience	▪ Executive sponsor ▪ Decision maker ▪ Business owner ▪ Power user ▪ Administrator	▪ Make sure the goal matches the audience (e.g. you wouldn't talk to your power user about the renewal) ▪ Always connect with multiple levels of people within each customer to minimize risk when people leave an organization

Even with the above considerations, how do you best prepare? You've already heard some great advice so here are more tips with a little twist:

▪ Ensure you're at least 75% prepared for the discussion – this is especially important for significant "moments of truth" or milestones along the customer journey, like executive business reviews. However, preparation is equally important for everyday interactions

(continued)

(*continued*)

with customers. By the way, if you're 100% prepared, then you've probably spent too much time preparing and won't be able to get all your other work done.

- Schedule calls for 25 minutes instead of 30, or 55 minutes instead of 60 so that both you and your customer have an opportunity to prepare for what's next in your day or take a short break. Your customers will love you for this too! Remember, if you don't end on time or early, it defeats the purpose.

- Check to see if the customer has responded to any recent relationship or transactional surveys. If so, you can personally thank them for positive feedback, or you can acknowledge negative feedback and continue conversations about how to improve their results and experiences.

- Verify if the customer is opening your recent emails – especially for product releases or upcoming events. If you can see they didn't open a recent release notification, you can say something like, "I'm sure you've been very busy and may not have seen our release last month, but there's a new feature that came out that your team has been asking for so I wanted to briefly highlight that new capability today before we talk about your upcoming renewal."

- When available, monitor their usage or adoption trends of your products and services. Access to telemetry data is not always possible or required to provide amazing customer experience, but it's a fantastic tool when available. If that data shows positive trends, congratulate them! If the data shows negative trends, plan to offer a follow-up conversation to get to the root cause of the decline (assuming that's not part of your original agenda).

- Confirm if the customer is engaged in other ways with your organization. Watch for things that can be signals for overall health, like submitting support tickets or participating in your community forums. Remember, no new support tickets could be a sign that they don't care enough to call for help and can be even worse than too many open support tickets. You may also find that customers who take advantage of programs like your community are healthier because they're making new product suggestions or asking for improvements to existing functionality. Keep an eye out for these insightful data points.

- Survey responses, usage, customer support ticket data, and community engagement could all be part of a broader overall Health Score as well. Rolling up this type of data into one objective Health Score is an easier way to prepare for calls and meetings since you can use a simple scoring scheme. At a glance, you can identify the potential root cause of declining health. You can easily see that the average number of support tickets have increased over the last four weeks compared to the prior four weeks. This can help you drive a better experience by using it as a conversation prompt. For example, "I noticed there had been an increase in your support tickets. So, I asked our team to do an analysis of the cause and get back to me." Now you can move to the topic you wanted to discuss, and the customer will likely be more amenable to the conversation.
- Remember to check the customer's website for announcements and press releases so you can congratulate them on other positive updates as well.

In the end, prepare for customer engagement by contemplating what you want from the interaction and what the customer wants from you. Consider your audience and ensure every time that you're bringing value to the conversation or in the email. By practicing some of these preparation best-practice fundamentals, you'll earn your customers' respect regardless of challenges on the horizon, they'll stay engaged with you in return, and you'll maximize the value of your partnership and your results.

The Art of Discovery: Asking the Right Questions to Get to the Heart of the Customer's Problem

Preparation and due diligence are the foundation of your journey as a Customer Success Manager. Every bit of information you learn about your potential or current customer is an investment that will eventually pay off. It is with that in mind that we compiled a long list of discovery questions we used at Gainsight for our own customer engagements. It was started years ago by our good friend Easton Taylor, whom we introduced you to in Chapter 3, and has grown to well over a hundred different questions. Below is a shortened sample of general discovery questions. You can find the expanded list at www.gainsight.com by searching under Resources for "Art of Discovery." We encourage you to create your own situational go-to questions to help ensure you are learning as much as you can about your customers.

General discovery:
1. Who is the customer?
2. Where are they in their journey as a company? Looking for an IPO?
3. What is the industry chatter?
4. What services or products do they provide or sell?
5. What is the purpose of the meeting? Who called it?
6. Where are they in their journey as your customer?
7. How long have they been your customer?
8. What is the customer's current satisfaction level?
9. What is the health of the relationship between you, your company, and your customer?
10. Have they attended any of your company-sponsored events?
11. Do they engage in your webinars or marketing materials?
12. Are they the right fit as a customer?

Finding the Right Questions and Asking the Questions Correctly

The skill of effectively questioning your customer is referred to as the "The Art of Discovery." Questions serve various purposes when connecting with potential clients and established customers. It is not just about attaining vital information that will help your customers get back on the road to wellness. The right questions asked at the right time, build a rapport that eventually enriches the relationship.

The individual who is asking the question is in control of the conversation and the environment. Whether they admit it or not, the customer wants your help. You would not be there if they were not seeking a remedy to their situation. A customer is looking for someone to believe in their vision. You must provide affirmation to their situation. That is a human-first skill. If they believe you, they are more than likely to feel safe and show their vulnerability. This trust opens the door to reveal the "pain points" of their business.

The content of your questions is vital in the art of discovery. How the questions are delivered is equally important. There is an old adage that says, "The prophecy is subject to the prophet." In other words, the message you bring to your customers could make them more successful and perhaps even save them. The wrong delivery and actions, however, can turn your green or yellow light customer into an at-risk, red customer. Customer Success is about customer experience. It is not just the tone and phrasing of your questions that help. One must also be careful not to communicate a personal message or agenda. Questions like "Are you sure you want to do this?" or "Do you think this is going to work?" are both examples of messages that indicate you do not believe in their ideas. It is better to be honest and more direct.

Lastly, your physical presence gives greater significance to your questions. While some prescribe to the soft skills of reading a room, human-first skills emphasize your manners, behavior, and demeanor despite what information you may gain from a customer's reaction. Now, let us begin the meeting.

The Meeting: Creating an Effective First Customer Experience

It is not uncommon for the first meeting with your customer to be virtual or over the phone. Sometimes this occurs near the end of the sales cycle. Most often, it happens after the customer signs a contract with your company, and maybe not until after initial implementation is completed. At some point along the early journey, you are assigned as the customer's CSM. It's an exciting milestone that can bring some uncertainty. Your company has entrusted you with a precious new account to ensure success for all. You are also the person your customer assumes will be competent, trustworthy, and capable of guiding them to their desired outcomes. As such, the very first impression you make is a critical one. While the next section describes an in-person meeting, there is much value to following nearly every suggestion even for a virtual conference. You may find that the tone and video presence will be similar, if not the same.

The Introduction aka "Being the Expert in the Room"

When you enter a room, you divulge a great deal about your character. Posture, smiles, soft eyes, and an open stance gives the impression of a willingness to help. Ask yourself, what is your body language telling everyone in the room? Be careful what you glean from the other people present. No matter what that body language may say about them, it is not to be used to your advantage. The emphasis is on making them a success, not making a sale.

Give a brief history of who you are, and who your team members are. Explain your role in your company and include your past professional experience that may seem relatable (i.e. I have been part of a Marketing team). Be sure to ask if there is anything more that the customer wants you to know about them and their company that may prove useful to the process.

Often, as a CSM, you are brought in during a business crisis. It is essential to find out if there is something that the customer believes or values as the most critical issue that they want to convey to you and your team. Allow the customer to share concerns and explain what their position is. This action gives the customer the ability to be heard and feel like they matter from the beginning of the meeting. It is a risk to ask, but it could yield unexpected benefits. The key lies in your ability to redirect the meeting and conversations to refocus on what the original goal was.

A key to any initial meeting is asking what makes the customer's product unique or different from similar products on the market? Also, what makes you different from your competition? Another valuable insight is to find out which competitor they may respect. These are open-ended questions. Give the customer time to answer with enough detail. It proves to the customer that you are not willing to make assumptions or poor choices. Ultimately, it shows that you are listening.

Every business has unique elements to it besides the products or services it offers. Find out what their top three unique elements are. Next, have them focus on their customers. Of all their customers, which ones do they value the most or are the most valuable? Ask what the top three reasons are that they believe their most valued or best customers conduct business with them. Are these the same reasons they stay with you as customers?

Lastly, discuss your customer's limitations. Every company has complaints. What are the three most common customer complaints about them? Do they know the most common reasons customers cite for leaving? Another subject to discuss is their future. What do they believe are the biggest challenges facing their customers? Ask them, "Do you believe your customers' expectations have changed recently or over the past five years?"

Moving Toward Identifying and Developing a Need

Hopefully, the client is now aware that you have their best interest at heart. In the next section, be mindful that the questions require direct answers. Sometimes the answers become rigid and lead to anxious situations. Tension can bring about a decline in the quality of the answers. It may be fruitful to give the customer time for composure and contemplation, ultimately leading to redirection and focus.

Be sure to discuss what are the actual or opportunity costs of their current problem. Stress to them your respect for their business insight. What do they think the savings would be if this issue were remedied? It is necessary for you to understand how their current problems affect other aspects of their business, including sales, costs, productivity, and overall morale. Moreover, you should know if there are any other areas of their business that are affected.

Part of any solution is finding out what has been done so that there is no redundancy. What solutions have they already tried and how successful were they? Do they believe there will be organizational resistance to changes that are made? The last thing to ascertain is whether there are any relevant issues that may assist the CS team in coming to a greater understanding of this issue. Trust and vulnerability can open your customers to share more vital information and make your job easier.

Understanding Aspirations and Goals

In this last section, you will want to acquaint yourself with your customer's immediate and future goals. Begin with what they have accomplished thus far. What do they credit for their current level of success? Do they believe those explanations will change in the future? If so, where do they go from here in terms of future improvements in performance? Another item to discover is how their priorities may have changed over time?

Have them tell you what their three most significant current priorities are. Do the priorities they described include opportunities for growth? Do they believe growth will come from existing customers versus new customers? Do they have a current strategy to achieve those opportunities? Changes can profoundly influence current strategies. Are there foreseeable changes or trends that could affect current strategies?

Often there are organizational or operational capabilities that they will need to strengthen to support their future strategies significantly. Can they identify them? If they had additional resources, which initiatives would they choose to advance? In this same train of thought, ask them "blue sky" questions such as "What more could you ask for if there was no chance of it being denied?"

As you finish your session with the customer, find out what risk management looks like for their company? What would organizational effectiveness look like? Which do they believe is better suited for their company? Lastly, how do they think their personal performance should be evaluated at the end of the year?

Challenging and Persuading the Customer

Customer Success Managers often find themselves in precarious situations concerning assessing what is best for the customer as they journey along their prescribed road to success. The need to be both persuasive and sometimes provocative go hand in hand, especially if the customer is headed down a road of imminent failure. If you don't already know it, consider yourself an authorized "movie-spoiler." In other words, you have an obligation to sound the warning trumpet to your customers, especially if you have seen the same doomed situation play out before with other customers. It is not an option to recuse yourself from this potentially difficult circumstance or believe you can approach it with an air of passivity. Instead, you must accept your trusted-advisor role with a confident duty, whether they want to hear it or not, and provide your customer with appropriate guidance as the situation warrants. Remember, your primary objective as a Customer Success Manager is to ensure your customer is attaining their desired outcome, which does not include failure. This might mean you having to outright tell your customer "no." Your customers will appreciate you, even if they disagree, because the motivation for your warning is in their best interests.

There are easy ways to challenge your customer and not appear rude while doing it. Try the "not advisable because . . ." instead of "no." This provides clarification for why you disagree with a particular point of view. Even better, say no without saying no. "Let me suggest a different approach here so we can talk through multiple solutions." Wherever possible, be fact based. You can argue against opinions but not so easily against facts. If you want to persuade your customer to use a different approach than what they are currently considering, use examples of other customers, ideally as similar to them as possible. Convey a "proven" approach that brings with it lower risk.

There is a myth that challenging your customer is simply a matter of being contrary or "pushing them." Truthfully, challenging your customer is more about persuasion than objection. What you message to your customers right after their purchase will be different than what you say to them at the time of renewal, and different when you are trying to convince them to buy more or adopt new product features. Tailor your messages to the current state of the customer. Doing so will yield the outcomes you and your customer are expecting.

●●●

In this chapter, we discussed why consolidating your data sources related to your customers is foundational to collaborating across different teams in your quest to create a customer-centric company. We also discussed tactical steps to prepare for customer interactions, asking the right questions, and understanding customer needs. Finally, we established how challenging and persuading the customer is critical to keeping the customer on the best path to success. In the next section, we delve into core tasks that help you manage, retain and grow your customers.

Endnotes

1. Avery, J., Fournier, S., and Wittenbraker, J. (2014). Unlock the mysteries of your customer relationships. *Harvard Business Review* (July–August 2014). Retrieved from: https://hbr.org/2014/07/unlock-the-mysteries-of-your-customer-relationships.
2. Ransbotham, S. and Kiron, D. (2018). Using analytics to improve customer engagement. *MIT Sloan Management Review* (January 2018). Retrieved from: https://sloanreview.mit.edu/projects/using-analytics-to-improve-customer-engagement/.

7 | Defining the Journey to Customer Outcomes

We live and work in the age of data. The ability to use the information gathered on customers for insight into your relationships with them is more important than ever before. Data is a powerful asset. You could say that data, next to your customers, is your most precious resource.

It is interesting that customers willingly provide you with this kind of access. They permit you to watch and analyze their usage of your product. They even give responses to surveys and participate in other data–gathering techniques. Why do they allow such intrusions into their business information? Your customers do this because, first, they feel safe and their information is protected. Second, they expect something in return. They have the *rightful* expectation that your company will safeguard their information and utilize all the data you have gathered to accelerate the delivery of success for them.

With all the knowledge provided by collected data comes serious responsibility. As a Customer Success Manager or the leader of the Customer Success team, you must harness the information, convert it into actionable insights, and proactively engage with your customers to achieve their outcomes and goals. Most of all, you must do this in a human-first manner, ensuring the safety of all the knowledge gathered and protecting your customer's vulnerabilities.

Using the knowledge and insights driven by data, you can draw out the expected path for your customers to get to their outcomes. This path can change from one customer to the other depending on a variety of factors. When customers go off their planned success-path, it's important to acknowledge it, communicate the plan to get back on the path and execute together to make it happen. This chapter delves into how you can create the desired journey and tailor it, depending on your customer segments. We'll also dive into tactics and examples of operationalizing the path to outcomes and desired milestones along the way in Chapter 8.

Customer Lifecycle, Journey Map, Customer Journey

The Lifecycle, the Journey Map, and the Customer Journey are three terms that have long been used interchangeably to describe the multi-staged paths that get your customers to their goals or outcomes. Unfortunately, the descriptive titles are close in nature, but their purposes are misunderstood. Each is a distinct entity with its own aim that should be defined and clarified.

We believe in the necessity of standardization for all Customer Success, which is one reason why we wrote this book. As Customer Success grows and evolves, there needs to be a foundation, a touchstone, that everyone can look to and reference. Without it, definitions are blurred and the industry becomes unfocused. Here is where we hope you will learn the proper definition of the Customer Lifecycle, a Journey Map, and the Customer Journey. You will also learn what your role as a CS professional is in each phase of the Customer Lifecycle, how to create a Journey Map for your customers, and how to navigate the Customer Journey.

Defining the Customer Lifecycle

In the business world, the Customer Lifecycle is a term that describes the entire process of managing a customer. You may have seen graphics like the ones in this chapter that represent the Lifecycle. Perhaps the circle illustration or the infinity symbol (Figures 7.1 and 7.2)? The Lifecycle has also been called the Customer Journey. However, with further study of examples, we see that the Customer Journey is now seen as a subset that exists within the Lifecycle.

Confused? Don't be. It will be explained. Remember that the Customer Success field is evolving. It is still young, and definitions will be clarified as it progresses.

No matter the industry or business you may be in, there is a commonly acknowledged methodology that every customer must pass through. Whether you are a tech company, SaaS, or you deal in on-premise software, customers go through recognizable phases of progress in their Lifecycle. There are typically five phases to the Customer Lifecycle and each phase has a purpose with the potential for success and failure. While the Lifecycle is a general mechanism, different companies may choose various terms and names for each phase. These are the most commonly named phases within the Lifecycle: Consider or Evaluation, Purchase, Onboarding, Adoption, Renewal, and/or Expansion or Churn.

> **Consider or Evaluation:** this is the phase where the customer compares products that could solve its business problems. The Marketing organization, and sometimes Sales, generally manages this phase. Marketing creates advertising and the environment that makes your product or service appealing. A potential customer reaches out through various avenues of contact. Then a Sales Rep will take the lead to try to produce a sale or purchase.
>
> **Purchase:** the purchase phase typically involves a choice of product or service and negotiations over a contract. While this phase is the domain of Sales, it may require the expertise of a Sales Engineer or even an experienced CSM in an advisory role. Your future customers could have special needs or demands that are placed in their contract or a Statement of Work which is also called an SOW. Once the contract is signed, and there is an exchange of funds, the transition begins. You will want the customer to move forward, onboard, and engage the product as soon as possible.
>
> **Onboarding:** typically the onboarding phase includes setting up and activating the people that will be using your product. In most companies, this phase is managed by an onboarding team or CSMs depending on the

product complexity. The phase ends with the customer being educated and adept at using your product or service.

Adoption: in this phase, customers are "adopting" the parts of the product that they are entitled to use by the terms of their purchase contract. Customer Success Managers usually lead customers during this phase. You will know if your customer is a success if they are achieving their business outcomes. When they do, they become a potential advocate on your behalf to other prospects and customers. This phase may also include customers buying more products, additional services, or buying more licenses or seats to your software or product from you. These are referred to as upsells, cross-sells, or expansions.

Renewal and/or Expansion: this is the phase where customers decide to continue and/or expand their relationship with your product or service. This phase, like Adoption, is often managed by CSMs. The goal is to learn as much as you can about your customers. If they are using your product well, then this indicates they are in good health and can potentially benefit from additional products or services that you may offer. That good health must be sustained by monitoring their health scores and nurturing the customer experience.

Churn: this is the phase where customers decide to end their relationship with your product or service. This phase, like Adoption, is managed by CSMs. If they decide to end the agreement and no longer use your product or service, it is necessary to find out the reasons for the churn. Do not try to ascertain the reason behind their departure on your own. Always try to use an unbiased third party who is skilled in debriefing your customer. The information is incredibly valuable. We'll discuss churn analysis in greater detail in Chapter 12. In the meantime, it should be your company's aim to make the offboarding process as simple as possible, for you and your departing customer. The idea is that you would like them to become a prospect again. Letting them depart with "class" may potentially increase the likelihood of their return as a customer in the future.

Customers travel through each phase or drop out of the Lifecycle completely, leading to a Churn. To be successful, however, every customer, no matter the company has to go through an Evaluation, a Purchase, an Onboarding, an Adoption, and hopefully a Renewal/Expansion, while avoiding Churn altogether. There are many ways to visualize the Customer Lifecycle: Figures 7.1 and 7.2 show two.

Figure 7.1   Example 1 Customer Lifecycle.

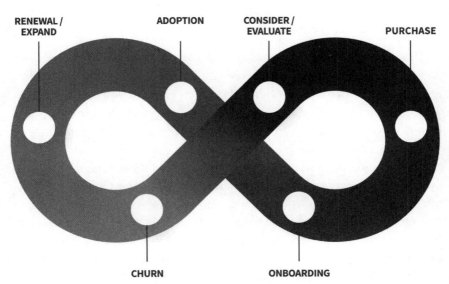

Figure 7.2   Example 2 Customer Lifecycle.

The Journey Map Defined

Within each phase of the Lifecycle lies the Journey Map. The Journey Map is a lean management technique. Its purpose is to devise a path for the customer from the sale, through implementation and adoption, then to full engagement, and, hopefully, retention. This map is a set of milestones that indicate advancement toward the overall goal of customer success. The markers, transitions, and events along the journey are set by the CS team to show the customer their progress along the way. With journey mapping, you will identify every step and every event. You may even be able to forecast potential problems because you thoroughly planned the customer's journey.

The Journey Map is not a new method or device. It has recently re-emerged within the recurring revenue business model with a different sense of purpose and urgency in its usage. The purpose of a Journey Map is multifold. The first is to closely monitor and actively manage every aspect of the Customer Journey. The best way to monitor a customer is along a predetermined path. The path you create centers on the goals and expectations of both your customers and your company. Every customer buys your product or service for a specific use that can be distilled into three questions.

- How can they make more money?
- How can they save money?
- Are they attempting to become efficient and save time?

Your company has expectations and goals for not just the customer's success, but for every team and every Lifecycle phase. Whatever the designated targets, the customer should be the center of your Journey Map. The expectations and goals are essential, and they must be reaffirmed and recorded properly for peace of mind of the customer, for the intentions of your teams, and to guarantee the continuity of care.

The second purpose of the Journey Map is to determine the best and optimal steps to get to those goals. With each set of steps, you must identify where different teams or organizations within your company become responsible for various tasks during each Lifecycle phase. The transitions from one team or organization to another are called **handoffs.** Most companies who are a recurring revenue business have quite a few handoffs in the Lifecycle. In a progressive Customer Success environment, there is no way to avoid it.

If you think about the Lifecycle of a customer, they could have up to a dozen or more people from your company involved in their journey in the first year alone. That can be overwhelming. Every Customer Success team using a Journey Map should use it as a standardized method of handoff from pre-sales to post-sales phases. Each handoff has the potential to erode the trust that was developed during the initial sales cycle. It can also prolong the time to value. There is much information that needs to transition from one group to the next. All the learned information about the customer must be smoothly communicated from handoff to handoff to sustain the momentum you gained during the sales cycle.

The truth is, customer handoffs set the quality standard for the rest of the Customer Journey. If the relationship starts on a wrong note, it is hard to get it back in tune. It is also not uncommon for a CSM to be assigned more accounts than they can handle. It is vital to keep your own emotions in check in these situations because you don't want your new customer to feel your anxiety as it may cause uncertainty at a critical point in your new relationship. It is essential to manage the entire journey, especially the handoff, in a way that builds confidence with the customer.

When the journey is defined clearly, make sure that you follow it. Map out the entire Customer Lifecycle and identify the different milestones that they are going to hit, along with the lifecycle stages, transitions, and events. This process will keep your teams aligned on the customer's priorities across Sales and Services handoffs. It will also ensure that you are executing in support of those use-cases. You can watch every step. This methodology, however, is not just for the internal use of you and your team. It is both for yourself and for your customers. A healthy customer is an informed customer. Creating a Journey Map prevents the increase in anxiety and an occurrence of "buyer's remorse." It ultimately enhances the customer experience.

How to Create the Journey Map

There are many ways to go about creating Journey Maps for your customers. The process begins with your CS team physically coming together to look at your customer base. Maybe you have a place in your business that the team can gather. Another thing to consider is to take your team off-site to a co-working space or conference room and get creative.

The next step is to find what tools can you use. Some people simply utilize a whiteboard. Others favor giant sticky notes, small post notes, or notes of all shapes and sizes. Another option is three by five cards. If there is a preferred methodology at your company that is established, utilize that. Often, mapping in a linear sequence is best.

Whatever you choose to do or whatever works well for you and your team, there are two critical parts. One is input. Sometimes it takes everyone getting a pen and writing down what they believe will be beneficial to the Journey Map. As you proceed through all the ideas, you find you can revisit them until you are confident they all apply to your customers. In fact, you may find that the Journey Map is not a one size fits all. You have to create various maps based on the type, size, or needs of the customer. The operation is not as important as the consensus. There are definite benefits to thinking through the process and doing it as a group makes a big difference.

The second critical part is to consider the customer's point of view. Create a map with the customer in mind. Think about them holistically from purchase to the realization of their goals. Consider if they interact or do business with other companies. Think about who their biggest competitors are. Next, contemplate the customer's culture and language within their company. Are there ideologies that they promote? Are there keywords that they use? These are highly important in your presentation of the Journey Map. Lastly, think about the moments on their journey that are relatable to them. As you go through this exercise, you will find that you can break it down into greater detail.

Like a road map, a Journey Map can have various routes to the same destination, which is renewal and/or expansion. However, each course is dependent on the customer, their size and segmentation, their desired outcomes and goals, and the speed at which they want to accomplish them. Also, remember that the customer will interact with different teams or organizations within your company during each phase. As you and the customer move through the Lifecycle, you will know they are ready to move on to the next phase by what they accomplish. However, it is not just about hitting the benchmarks. It is also about managing the Lifecycle to create an experience in which every customer feels there are possibilities and accomplishments. In Figure 7.3 we highlight an example of the milestones you might consider building out in your own Journey Maps for your customers.

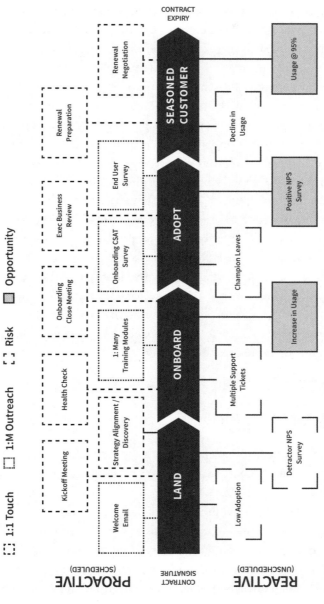

Figure 7.3 An example Journey Map.

When your Lifecycle and Journey Maps are not clear, your interactions with your customers will likely appear haphazard, without intent or without ownership. The symptoms can be a poor transfer of knowledge from one team to another within the company. Another is repetitive manual actions that cannot scale as the customer count increases. Such a disorganized execution can produce an inconsistent experience from one customer to another. Eventually, the symptoms become detrimental to the overall health of your customers. Because of a lack of clarity, direction, and ownership, customers inadvertently receive *only* what they ask for, not what you know they need most. Ultimately, none of these activities will get your customers additional value from your service or product.

The antidote to these symptoms of disorder goes back to creating an organized, consistent Journey Map within each Lifecycle phase for your customers. The Journey Map enables your customer-facing teams to execute the individual Customer Journey with precision so that your customers know exactly what to expect working with your teams.

Establishing a Journey Map starts with identifying clear customer segments. Journey Maps are not the same for every customer or customer segment. They will, however, have common markers that must be hit during each phase of the Lifecycle. Each Journey Map is largely dependent on how your customers are separated or segmented.

Segment Your Customers

As stated in Chapter 6, customer data is an incredible asset in managing the customer relationship. One tool to organize that data is known as segmentation. In the book *Data Mining in the CRM Framework,* the authors define segmentation as "the process of dividing the customer base into distinct and internally homogeneous groups in order to develop differentiated marketing strategies according to their characteristics."[1] The homogenous groups are subgroups of existing and even potential customers that share certain identified market traits. Utilizing this information can, as the authors suggest, "support an 'individualized' and optimized customer management throughout all the phases of the customer lifecycle, from the acquisition and establishment of a strong relationship to the prevention of attrition and the winning back of lost customers."[2]

The segmentation tool can also help you deliver what each type of customer needs in a way that's affordable for the company. Separating your customers into logical groups is critical for optimizing the efficiency of your Customer Success Management team. Segmentation will also help define the relative value of each customer and, ultimately, determine your engagement or touch model. In the end, segmenting your customers allows you to allocate resources to the right customers at the right time.

There are many ways to segment your customers, and it will vary from business to business. Every time you divide your customer base to organize it better, you increase your ability to manage your customers more effectively. So, how do you properly segment your customers?

One of the most impactful tools in segmentation is referred to as value segments. Value segments are classifications of customers that hold the *most value* to your company. There are five common distinctions: Contract Value, Customer Size, Industry, Brand, Customer Advocate.

Contract Value: segmenting by contract value is a simple way that ranks customers, from highest to lowest, by how much they pay your company. Many companies see this as the first and only criterion for segmentation. Unfortunately, such a narrow view can minimize the "human-first" component of Customer Success.

Customer Size: the second segmentation is based on customer size. Sometimes this is referred to as "white space segmenting." Customer size does not necessarily mean the overall size of the company. Properly, it should refer to the size of the overall opportunity each customer has for greater expansion and recurring revenue.

Industry: organizing your customer base by industry can be beneficial. For example, suppose your company's solution is the perfect fit for technology firms. Your company, however, is trying hard to break into Financial Services. You may find that your current Financial Services customers suddenly have a higher strategic value than your technology customers.

Brand: a brand is the identity or image that makes a product or company unique. That same brand concept contributes to the value of a customer. That is why companies in your industry aggressively compete for the big logo customers because landing the big logo typically leads to more big names and highly valued customers.

Customer Advocate: these are your very best customers. They have great customer health, excellent use of your product, and probably are already or are going to be long term. They are customers that would give you the best "references" to potential customers. It's logical, then, to place a higher specific value on them for the purpose of segmentation.

Another way to segment customers is to organize them by demographics, geographics, or a combination, called firmographics. The first is business size, either by the number of employees or annual revenue. Next, maybe the company location (i.e. inner-city Chicago versus rural Utah). Another is the industry in which the customer exists. Is it SaaS, tech-based, or brick and mortar? There are even further segmentations that can be used, such as the technologies and software utilized by the targeted companies.

Each of the previously mentioned segmentation models are based on your relationship with the customer, either to their size, place, or type of business. Consider a way to efficiently use segmentation concerning your product or service. Each segmented group should be defined by their need from your product or service and your ability to serve them cost-effectively. For each segment, you need to designate distinct markers of development that your customers accomplish after they buy your product or service on their Lifecycle path to achieving their business outcomes.

A more sophisticated way to think about segments is based on your customer's needs. For example, if you were Dropbox, you can segment your customers based on the requirement for storage solutions, productivity and sharing tools, or support levels. Another level of segmentation is your customer's sophistication using your product or service. How proficient are they in its use? There is even a segmentation based on behavior. Knowing your customer's behavior is especially beneficial when it comes to determining customer health. For instance, are your current customers interacting with your product or solution in a manner that may indicate they could benefit from expanding their current solution? Alternatively, is this customer at risk of churning from your solution?

In a 2019 Gainsight survey that benchmarked the CS industry, more than 800 respondents shared their top three metrics that dictate how they segment their customers (Figure 7.4). As suspected, the three most common, in order, were contract value (ARR), customer size, and growth potential. The numbers indicate that the most preferred method of

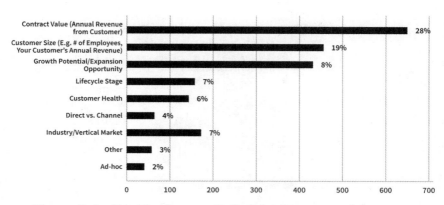

Figure 7.4   Results from a Gainsight Survey on how companies segment their customers.

segmenting customers relates to potential expansion opportunities, which includes growth and company size.

Here is a consolidated list of variables to consider when segmenting:

- revenue
- Customer Lifecycle stage
- maturity stage
- growth potential
- geography/territory
- industry/vertical
- direct/channel
- use–case
- customer health
- CSM–skill required
- security clearance
- temporary TLC touch model
- strategic relationship
- product.

Certainly, there are many attributes that might drive your segmentation. Do not, however, make this process too complex when starting off. Keep it simple with maybe three to four segments, with the possibility of a few sub-segments. Remember, you want new customers to easily and logically fit into one of those relatively small number of groups. Also, you'll

Figure 7.5   Segments based on revenue.

need to consider how to explain it all to the rest of your company. An example of a simple and common way of segmentation is based on revenue. Segmenting by Annual Recurring Revenue usually divides the customer base into three segments (Figure 7.5). These are Enterprise, Mid-Market, and Small Business.

> **Enterprise:** this is the segment with the highest revenue per customer. In most companies, the Enterprise segment has a small number of customers (10–20% of the customers by count) but constitutes 50% or more of the revenue. Companies often refer to this segment as the Strategic or Global tier as well.
>
> **Mid-Market:** the next segment in terms of the highest revenue per customer. This segment typically forms the next 30–40% of customers by count, bringing in a proportionate amount of revenue.
>
> **Small Business:** this is the "long tail" of really small customers with really small revenue per customer but together forming a meaningful percentage of revenue. Given the volume of customers in this segment, it's hard to economically manage these customers' success. Hence, most companies either leave this segment unmanaged or use technology to monitor health and automate outreaches, wherever possible.

How you choose to segment your customers is up to your company, but it is preferable in most businesses to use the same segment definitions across all functions or teams (e.g. Sales, Marketing, Customer Success, Support).

However, if CSM efforts do not align effectively with designated segments, it's wise to consider developing a different segmentation model than the rest of the company. For example, apply a CS-specific segmentation model when some customers within the same segment require more advanced technical or strategic advice, in-depth knowledge of a use-case or product, or geographically convenient in-person support. Segmenting not only allows you to divide your customers for cost-effective and efficient management purposes, but it also enables you to produce accurate Journey Maps that reflect the specific needs and priorities of a customer. Segmentation and Journey Maps go hand in hand to help create a Customer Journey filled with experiences that reinforce their choice of your product or service.

The Customer Journey

You have, thus far, learned what the Customer Lifecycle is with all its distinct phases of Consider or Evaluation, Purchase, Onboarding, Adoption, Renewal, or Churn. You know that the Journey Map is a capable tool that provides a selected path with different milestones, transitions, and events across the Lifecycle phases. You also know how to create the Journey Map that matches the customer's desired goals, as well as their segmentation needs. This Journey Map will keep your teams aligned on the customer's priorities across Sales and Services handoffs. It will also ensure that you are executing in support of those use-cases. Moreover, you will find the Journey Map is both for yourself and your customers. It manages their anxieties, concerns, and emotional levels to produce positive experiences in what we call the Customer Journey.

The Customer Journey is deeply connected to the emotional part of the created Journey Map and the Customer Lifecycle. You could say it is the result of the experiences produced by both of them. It's what the customer actually goes through as compared to the desired Journey Map. The Customer Journey is the "actual" while the Journey Map is the "desired" – and in an ideal world, they are the same! It is interesting how powerful these experiences along the Customer Journey can be. Allison Pickens, Chief Operating Officer of Gainsight, said in her Pulse 2019 Keynote address that she believed that the "treadmill of technology has eliminated every autonomous moment we experience so that we rarely exercise the muscle of reflection." Her statement caused us to pause and ponder how this relates to the Customer Journey.

In the technology and software industry, we create products and services with the intent of making our customers more successful. It is fascinating, however, that these same products can also remove the ability to feel human, connected, and even can make us more fearful than secure. Allison later went on to write an online article based on her Keynote speech. She stated that "Products today reinforce and take advantage of our basest emotions – especially feelings of inadequacy and fear of missing out or being left behind. They erode behaviors we once valued and that I would argue, make us more human: independent thinking, deep consideration, and control over our actions. Products today don't speak to our highest human nature. Technology has become first; humanity, second."[3] How, then, do you create an environment where the customer is moving towards their goals? Allison suggested countermeasures and principles that fulfill a human-first standard.

You, as the Customer Success Manager or the leader of a Customer Success team, know that when the customer buys your product or service, they purchased it for a specific use. What if by using your product or service, the customer not only found success, but it created a journey that caused positive experiences and elicited our most human emotions? What if you could accomplish this by creating "interventions" in each Lifecycle phase and then built them into your Journey Maps? What if you could even leverage the data that you collect on your customers to input these situations at the right time and right place along with the accompanying emotions?

Not only are you accomplishing the customer's goals and generating responses that will ultimately connect the experiences, you are building a strong, educated customer while creating a strong bond with the product, you, and your company.

Endnotes

1. Tsiptsis, K.K. and Chorianopoulos, A. (2011). *Data Mining Techniques in CRM*. Wiley, Kindle Edition: Kindle locations 202–203.
2. Ibid., Kindle locations 194–196.
3. Pickens, A. (2019). 5 Principles of Human-First Products, Gainsight, 21 May 2019. Retrieved from: https://www.gainsight.com/blog/5-principles-of-human-first-products/.

8

Operationalize Your Customer Journey with Moments of Truth

In the previous chapter, "Defining the Journey to Customer Outcomes," you were presented with the idea that collecting data on your customer allows you to manage your customers' outcomes with the use of tools such as the Journey Map. Combining a concrete Customer Lifecycle and a clearly defined Journey Map will result in delivering a complete Customer Journey.

With these assets, you can better manage and align expectations, goals, and emotional experiences because you have minimized any surprises. The experiences turn into customer lessons. They can be meaningful, reaffirmed, and even recorded, just like any other goal or objective. You can also, through monitoring and guidance, align the customer with the product expectations as to what it really can and cannot do, producing a positive emotional outcome.

Once you, the Customer Success Manager, know and understand the customer's objectives and the "why," you can frame *all* of the post-sales tasks around those goals, including the experiences of what are called "Moments of Truth."

Identifying Your Moments of Truth

Within the Journey Map, there will be multiple interactions and experiences with you and your product that the customer can identify with. For the sake of the Journey Map, you need to identify the most critical of these interactions and experiences called "Moments of Truth." In the book *Customer Genius,* the author, Peter Fisk, wrote that these "Moments of Truth," were "meaningful experiences [that] are about relevant and distinctive interactions."[1] Instead of keeping the customer searching, you create an environment that gives them freedom and assurance to explore your product, its features, and other services you offer, enhancing the Customer's Journey.

These Moments of Truth are "make-or-break" situations, where a customer commits to the outcome emotionally, taking it as a sign of whether their partnership with you will be successful. Using these Moments, you can focus your team's efforts on achieving the intended outcomes for the customer's business at each marked moment on the Customer Journey. For each stop on the Journey Map, there must be desired Moments of Truth or MoTs.

Business-to-Consumer (B2C) companies have been thinking about MoTs for a long time. Checking into a hotel at the front desk is a critical MoT. It typically sets the tone for how you experience the rest of your stay at that hotel. Another example is when you experience issues with your cable-service at home and you call the cable company to resolve the issue. Their treatment of you and the situation helps you decide whether you will continue to be a customer or if you will recommend the cable company to your friends and family. In 2005, A.G. Lafley, Chairman, President and CEO of Procter & Gamble, a global B2C brand, revised the definition of Moments of Truth into three parts.[2]

1. When the customer is looking at a product. This can be in-store or online.
2. When the customer actually purchases the product and uses it.
3. When customers provide feedback about the product. They share it with the company as well as their friends, colleagues, and family members.

Many years ago, there was a pivotal business book written by Jan Carlzon, the former CEO of Scandinavian Airlines. Its title was the same title as our current subject matter, *Moments of Truth*.[3] Carlzon believed that a company should be customer-centric. He stated, "Any time a customer comes into contact with any aspect of your business, however remote, they have an opportunity to form an impression."

Lafley and Carlzon reaffirmed the concept that "ANYTIME" a customer comes into contact with your business, you have an opportunity to form a lasting impression that they will want to share with others. That should be an incentive to take every opportunity to create Moments of Truth.

The MoT should have nothing to do with your product or your needs. Peter Fisk put it this way. Moments of Truth are much more than "just consistent delivery across all the different touchpoints – they're about ensuring that the journey is connected and coherent, consistent and complete. On top of this, it's about bringing it (the journey) to life, making it distinctive, and relevant, and ultimately adding value at every point along the way."[4] In other words, the MoT will make sense to the customer, even if they had bought and were using a competitor's product. Also, when it happens, your customer will know and their perspective, in the end, is the most important one.

If this is your first time defining your Moments of Truth, start small. Identify just a few MoTs that you believe will resonate with both your company and your customer. Constructing a complete Customer Journey is a valuable but massive project. To aid you, there are eight MoTs that are critical and advantageous for long-term customer success (see Figure 8.1).

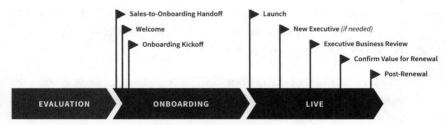

Figure 8.1   Example Moments of Truth in your Customer Lifecycle.

Sales-to-Onboarding Handoff

A prospective customer has been in a sales cycle with multiple members of your sales team for days, weeks, or even months. Now, they are ready to sign the contract and become a customer. Suddenly, they are introduced to a brand-new set of people – your company's Onboarding Team, Support Services, and CSM. The customer will go through a feeling of uncertainty. They will wonder if they can trust all the new people. They will question if the post-Sales teams know their business well enough. Even more, the customer will want to know if they will have to repeat everything they told the Sales team for the past few months. This feeling is very natural and very human. Your customer's anxiety and fears need to be calmed. You, as their CSM, will be responsible for alleviating their concerns quickly, so prepare accordingly.

A critical milestone is the Sales-to-Onboarding handoff. This first interaction must be done right to ensure a smooth transition for the customer. You want the customer to leave the first interaction with a feeling of confidence in the new relationships. There should be a sense of understanding and that they believe that all the new people involved "get" them. Moreover, your preparation efforts should give them the security of a "good start."

Typically, as soon as a customer signs a contract, your Sales team will mark the deal or opportunity in your CRM as a closed-win. There are a few steps that you should follow as a Customer Success Manager. First, schedule a call with the Sales Rep who owned the deal and/or the Sales Engineer to understand the business context and customer stakeholders. You can also send an internal questionnaire to individuals in your company who were actively involved in the sales process. It will include relevant questions and topics about the customer that you'll need to capture before your first meeting with them. Here are some example topics that you should talk through with the Sales team as part of the handoff:

- General customer information like the company's business model, the target users (group and/or department) for your product, the definition of success for *their* customers, etc.
- Key stakeholders including the executive sponsors and adoption champions, the main points of contact, administrators if they have been identified, and their competency levels, if known.

- Data quality and availability, if applicable to your product or services.
- IT and security requirements including if the IT team has been involved or advised of the project, security requirements/processes required for data access, release process for new products (and any blackout dates), etc.
- Any business-imposed timelines/deadlines associated with this project.
- Sales contract details including the number of products, licenses, etc. that were purchased, if any paid support plan was chosen, any integrations purchased, if applicable, etc.

Lastly, capture the notes in a repository system where they can be stored for future reference and shared with others in the organization. While this may seem like a "no brainer" for anyone using a CRM system, the truth is that companies aren't collecting, storing, and using data to the best of their abilities. Without proper storage and sharing capabilities, the information will not be properly used and therefore it will not add value to your organization.

Welcome the Customer and Onboarding Kickoff

The first call or meeting with the customer sets the tone for future expectations. So, it is vital to get right. You want the customer to leave the initial interaction believing the process you have given them will achieve their desired business outcomes. You also want them to understand the next steps in their journey and who will be a part of it. Lastly, the customer wants to know that all new persons they encounter from your company have taken the time to learn about them beforehand, so they don't have to repeat themselves. Simply, it's not your customer's job to educate you if the customer has already invested time conveying pertinent information to your Sales Reps or others from your company. In other words, you have to **nail the handoffs!**

In the case of a high-touch engagement, the Customer Success Manager or Onboarding team will start by scheduling a call or meeting with the Executive Sponsor. The purpose of the call is to make sure you validate the key business outcomes and the project plan for onboarding your product or service to them. It is also important to invite the Account Executive to the call to maintain continuity from the pre-sales process. After the call, a welcome email should be sent from your CS executive and company CEO to the customer. The CSM or project manager should also send a follow-up email capturing the notes from the meeting, recapping the project plan, and the next steps.

Launch or Go-Live

After going through onboarding, the process culminates in your customer getting access to your software and logging in for the first time. It's a critical Moment of Truth because it shapes the initial perceptions of your product or service. Those initial perceptions are very hard to change. It is imperative, then, to make sure that your customers have a memorable launch experience. You want the customer's primary decision-maker to leave the launch stage with the knowledge that they are set up to achieve all their business objectives. You want them to believe that they will accomplish everything that was agreed upon. You also want them to be secure in the understanding of who is responsible for the next steps in their journey. Most of all, you want them to see the impact you, your team, and your product has on their business.

As your customers leave the launch or go-live stage, they should know how to use your product effectively. If they have questions, they should be confident that there is a process or a contact person to help remedy the situation. When using the product, they should experience a sense that it is going to make their work easier. Share usage data that will emphasize they are on the prescribed path of success.

Most go-live launches involve some type of training for the customers, often online or virtual. If the training includes some hands-on exercises, that's even better. Best-in-class go-live launches include some childlike joy to keep the end-users engaged. A favorite example of this is when a customer hid some "Easter eggs" in their implementation of Gainsight. These Easter eggs were simply small clues that users could find *only* if they paid attention to your training!

New Customer Executive or Champion

Changes are part of every business. One such change is when your primary or executive business sponsor at the customer leaves the company or changes their role. This should be considered an immediate risk to your long-term engagement. This type of change usually means a new sponsor will take their spot and likely have a new set of priorities that they care about.

Understanding when these role changes happen, reaching out to the new executive, and quickly identifying any new priorities can make or break the future of your partnership with the customer. You want the new executive to feel like your company is genuinely interested in their personal and business success. If you are going to create a long-term partner, then there are some steps to ensure this happens.

With a new executive comes new executive priorities. Invest the time to understand these priorities. Next, you must find a way to convey that you want them to achieve their business outcomes as soon as possible. Timeliness is critical in this situation. Contact the customer to verify the change to the executive sponsor's position. In that same call or email, ask for an introduction to the new sponsor. Now, make that call!

You also need to inform your own company. Update the CRM system with the new sponsor's name and role. Schedule a meeting between the new sponsor and leaders of all your teams involved in the customer's account. The point of the meetings is not to just introduce your teams. You want to reaffirm the relationship, inform them of all that was accomplished up to the current date, and identify their future goals. The new sponsor may have some heavy or unexpected demands. The new customer executive needs to know that you have their best interests at heart. Solidify the relationship quickly.

While you are working on building an alliance with this new executive sponsor, you should be investigating what happened to the previous one. If they left your customer's employment, find out where the former executive went. Notify Sales where and with what company the executive ends up, especially if they were having a favorable experience with your company. Leverage that connection. It can be a new sales opportunity for your company.

Business Reviews: For the Executive and More

Some of the most effective ways to advise your customers of their health status and overall progress are with Quarterly Business Reviews (QBRs),

Executive Business Reviews (EBRs), and automated health reports or value readouts. It shows your customers that they are moving toward the objectives and targets they defined with you. It's important to note that there is not an imperative for these types of meetings to happen quarterly. Many companies call them Executive Business Reviews, or simply Business Reviews. They are conducted sometimes once, or twice a year, or even as frequently as every month.

Health status reports, when delivered during EBRs, are an essential part of an effective Customer Lifecycle. There is real value in illustrating to your customer where they stand, especially when it's done well and with a clear purpose. The goal here is to get the customer to take recommended actions based on their health, and not just get them to read the report. Some CS teams reserve using health reports only during face-to-face meetings, such as EBRs, because reports often need interpretation leading to action.

Here is a scenario: you have worked diligently to onboard the customer with your product. You have been successful, thus far, at getting the customer to adopt your product. They may even be achieving at least part of the business outcomes that they desired from you. What if you haven't been able to make sufficient progress with your customer and now you need the sponsor's help to remove certain organizational obstacles? An excellent place to advocate for assistance is at an EBR.

Who Should Attend?

An EBR is also a great forum to celebrate the value delivered thus far or to discuss the obstacles to value delivery. It is typically a meeting or a call attended by various customer stakeholders. For it to be a true EBR, however, there needs to be "executive" involvement. It would be best if you had senior representatives, typically VP and above, from the customer attend.

It also includes multiple functions from your own company attending – Customer Success, Sales, and Services. Representation from your company shows an "all in" agenda. You want the customer's executives to leave the EBR understanding the value they have achieved so far and believing in the steps they will take next. You especially want them to trust you as a strategic partner in moving forward. Even more, you need to see that their management is equally invested.

Pro-tip: consider rescheduling the EBR if no executives can attend or cancel at the last moment. It's called an *executive* business review for a reason. Nick Mehta, CEO of Gainsight, wrote in a blog post about this concept of "Progressive EBRs" in which EBRs are handled in phases described as parts of a dinner.[5] First, try preparing with a pre-EBR. Preparation and due diligence are great investments that eventually pay off. Remember, you don't have much time with the executives. You want to make sure you maximize the little time you can get with them. There are a few things you can put together beforehand to be more efficient during the meeting.

The Agenda

The typical agenda for an EBR should begin with introductions, especially if it's the first EBR or there are new participants. You will also need to give a short background or update about your company. This should cover things like new organization changes and new financial updates. The customer will want to know about funding rounds, mergers, and acquisitions as it shows your financial strength and stability.

If there are new product releases, consider giving a demonstration of your product or service, especially if there are new stakeholders. What you need to understand as a Customer Success Manager or CS executive is that the partnership shows progress and value delivered. Remind your customer of the progress and value delivered thus far with any ROI studies or assessments you have conducted.

The next item to discuss is the product roadmap. Explore their adoption progress and talk about customer case studies. Let the customer know all the implementation or Services Project Updates that are scheduled or happening at the present moment.

Ultimately, as the Customer Success Manager, you need to make sure there's enough value in your EBRs for the Executives to keep attending them.

Conducing the EBR

Right before the meeting begins, check to see that everything is live and working. Check the dial-in system, video connections, the projector, and the Wi-Fi. Make sure there are good whiteboard markers available. Many executive meetings can lose half of their designated time to technical problems. Start the session fast and with energy. Position yourself properly by standing up and moving to the front of the room. This move will increase the level of energy in the room. Try to skip the self-introductions. They can waste time if individuals decide to take ten minutes to give their LinkedIn biography. One creative way to accomplish it quickly is to have a mass introduction. You as the CSM or your CS executive should introduce everyone from your side, and one person from the client should do their introductions. You can turn 15 minutes of intros into a 2-minute drill!

First Course

The next phase can be called the First or "Appetizer Course." Here is a really important tip. Let's call it a must-do! You will likely only get through one or two topics and maybe three or five slides with executives because most will leave within the first 30 mins of your meeting. A great way to efficiently communicate the most important points of your meeting is to use an Executive Summary. Think of an Executive Summary as your entire presentation captured on one slide. It allows you to convey the most important points in just a few minutes. Use a bullet list format because it is easier to parse through when people don't have much time.

There are many ways to write a great Executive Summary. A common situation in a CSM's life is when you are trying to highlight a major problem, your proposed solution, and perhaps wins from already implementing the solution. Write your Executive Summary with three sections that talk about:

1. Acknowledging the problem – the current situation, and associated facts that prove it's a problem.
2. Illustrating the impact of not solving the problem (potential cost or time loss or savings), root causes of the problem, and barriers to solving the problem.
3. Calling out the actions suggested to solve the problem; if you've already taken the actions, call out learnings or wins from executing the solution.

Generally, in the "Appetizer Course," your senior executives and the Working Team are present. Utilize the first 30 minutes to articulate the company's strategic objectives related to the project. Advise and help your team, especially your own company executives, to prep in advance in an attempt to limit their "airtime" during the EBR. Most executives *love* to talk!

Next, have the customer project owner do an update in front of the customer executives. Hopefully, the news is good and affirms the positive momentum. If the report is not "great," do not shy away from it. Your customer wants honesty and transparency. It will do more harm than good if you keep anything from them. Next, have the most senior person from your side of the partnership share news, especially regarding the customer's momentum. Challenge the exec, if necessary, with advice on what more both companies could be doing together to mature faster.

Second Course

The Second or "Main Course" of an EBR involves the Working Team only. Most executives do not have the bandwidth to spend hours in a meeting such as this. This part of the EBR can take between one to two hours. The Main Course is the part of the meeting where most of the Business Review happens. Most of the topics discussed above are typically on the agenda of an EBR.

Third Course

The Third or "Dessert" phase of an EBR is when the Working Team coordinates the next steps. This portion of the EBR, which should last no more than 20 to 30 minutes, is when you and your team take the executive's strategic objectives and convert them into actions. You want them to be implemented in your product in collaboration with the customer team. For example, Figure 8.2 shows strategic objectives for the customer on the left side. These are from the intro by the executive in the "Appetizer" course. The action-plan on the right of the graphic is from the "Main" course.

STRATEGIC OBJECTIVES	ACTIONS
• Reduce time required to prepare for customer and internal meetings by 25% • Migrate 20% of our customer base from Platform 1 to Platform 2	• Bring data source 1, 2 and 3 into Gainsight • Use email automation in Gainsight to replace email 1 and email 2 that are manually sent by CSMs • Create a Success Plan in Gainsight to track progress of migration for each customer • Create a dashboard showing % of customers migrated and customers in progress and risks to migration

Figure 8.2   Example format for making Executive Business Reviews action-oriented.

Follow-up

Finally, make sure you are using the momentum from the EBR to make rapid progress. Always send an email with a meeting follow-up report and a "thank you" note during the same day, if possible. Include a shared EBR deck in PDF form along with your notes from the meeting. You can also place these items in your CS platform, CRM system, or wherever you store notes that are shared across the company. Anyone who has contact with your customer should have access to that information.

One last step is to create a "Success Plan." A Success Plan is a shareable set of tasks and next steps that both your company and the customer can jointly work on. We will cover Success Plans in more depth in Chapter 11.

Renewals

There's a common saying in the Customer Success world that if the customer is successful in adopting and receiving outcomes from your product or service, the renewal becomes a non-event. While the spirit of the statement is 100% true, a renewal Moment of Truth still requires careful preparation before and after the renewal commitment.

Let's go back for a moment and focus on what a renewal is. The renewal is and always will be a sales transaction. It can happen in one of two ways.

The first is explicit, as with a signed contract. That means you need a signature to continue the customer's business agreement with your company. The second way is implicit, as with an auto-renewal or "non-opt-out" agreement. Auto-renewal is often referred to as an "evergreen" contract. It does not need a signature when the contract expires and will automatically renew unless your customer informs you they are leaving. Your job as a Customer Success Manager is to make the renewal a non-event by ensuring the customer will always renew.

Contemplate this scenario: your customer is a healthy customer, but they have not been communicating with you as much. You are certain, however, that the upcoming renewal will be a non-issue because of their past usage and positive NPS scores. They have an EBR a month before the contract expiration date. What should you do?

Don't wait until the renewal date to communicate on the commercial terms with the customer. At least 120 days before the renewal, reach out to the customer. One opportunity is to make it a part of an EBR and discuss the value delivered to date, as well as how the partnership can continue to flourish. If there are any concerns or red flags raised, you have some time before the actual renewal to course-correct. At scale, this can also be done by digital outreaches.

The ideal outcome is for the customer to believe in the value of the tool, product, or service you provide. The proven value enables them to make a case to their internal decision-makers for its continued use, or they will be able to make that case in two to three months. In the scenario above, the EBR is just a month before contract expiration. It is advised that in the future, you move the EBR to the recommended 120-day period.

After the renewal paperwork is completed, close the loop with the customer. You should send a short note to the customer's executive, and the Working Team, thanking them for their continued partnership. For your low-touch customers, you could use an automated email to thank the customer for their renewed commitment and offer a conversation to plan out details. You want the customer to feel excited about the possibilities of what they can achieve. They should also believe that you and your teams are ready to help make their goals a reality.

●●●

This chapter gave you some actionable ideas on how to bring your Customer Journey to life by effectively managing your Moments of Truth. We shared some commonly seen Moments of Truth in the Customer Success world and how to best prepare and deliver those MoTs. See below for a step-by-step summary. In the next chapter, we'll discuss how to define your Health Scores and your tech-touch strategy to further increase visibility and insights into your customers.

Must Do's and Must Haves for a Successful Customer Journey

Operations
1. Affirm Lifecycle stages.
2. Determine segmentation delineator(s).
3. Define touch model for each segment (high, med, low/tech).
4. Identify critical customer stakeholders.
5. Identify Moments of Truth and key milestones.
6. Create outreach templates.
7. Create playbooks.
8. Define calls-to-action and threshold triggers.

Data
1. Segmentation variable.
2. Initial contract date.
3. Most recent contract date.
4. Renewal date.
5. Most recent contract term.
6. Auto renew (Y/N).
7. Segment name (or touch model name).
8. Moments of Truth and milestones.
9. Outreach email templates.

Endnotes

1. Fisk, P. (2009). *Customer Genius*. Capstone Publishing Ltd.
2. Hyken, S. (2016). The new moment of truth in business. *Forbes* (9 April 2016). Retrieved from: https://www.forbes.com/sites/shephyken/2016/04/09/new-moment-of-truth-in-business/#3fac6d2d38d9.

3. Carlzon, J. (1987). *Moments of Truth*. New York, NY: Ballinger Publishing Company.
4. Fisk, P. (2009). *Customer Genius*. Capstone Publishing Ltd, p. 216.
5. Mehta, N. (2019). How to Put the 'Executive' Back in Executive Business Review, 12 August 2019. Retrieved from: https://www.gainsight.com/blog/how-to-put-the-executive-back-in-executive-business-review/.

9

Using Customer Health Scores to Manage Your Customers

In the previous chapter, you were presented with the key moments in your Customer Journey that leave a lasting impression in your customers' minds – "Moments of Truth." As your customers go through their Customer Journeys, they keep sharing signals with you on how they are doing and how they are feeling. In this chapter, we will show you how to use the concept of Health Scoring to capture these signals, make sense of them, and leverage them to successfully manage your customers. We'll highlight different types of Health Scores and introduce frameworks that you can use to tweak to fit your company's needs.

Health Scores: How to Know If Your Customers Are Doing Well

One of the most often discussed topics in Customer Success is the notion of Health Scoring. It's based on the idea that your customers are constantly, implicitly or explicitly, giving you "signals" of how they are doing with your product or service. Customer Health Scoring is the concept that you can integrate together these various signals about your clients in order to quantify your customer base. Is it that simple? The easiest way to understand the concept of your customers' health is by drawing parallels to your personal health.

As a child, you are developing your immunity and more prone to illnesses. In that same manner, customers in their early days of using your product or service are at risk of needing a lot more attention to find value in your offering.

As you grow up, you are very active, go to the gym often, and are mostly in excellent health. Occasionally, however, there will be a small health issue. You may break a bone or two and need to be nursed back to health. It is no different for customers. Some get off to a good start, will adopt your product or service, and derive good value but will likely face some small health concerns. It could be a product bug that hampers adoption. There could be a change in executives that may impact business priorities and, hence, how their teams use your product or service.

As an adult, your priorities change, and you develop habits that affect personal health. Maybe you are smoking too much or not exercising as often as you should. Customers go through similar ups and downs with their use of your product or service.

Defining Health Scores

The Customer Health Score provides a consistent and shared view of where you are or are not providing your customers with value and positive experiences. From your customer's standpoint, it is an indication of whether they are getting value from your product and if they enjoy working with your company and product. From the vendor's standpoint, it equips you to increase retention, expansion, and advocacy in your customer base.

Most organizations, however, struggle with creating Health Scores. It is challenging to establish a steady, cross-functional method to identify and visualize data-driven measures of your customer's health. Some companies oversimplify their customer health into one metric or swing the exact opposite direction of including too many metrics. Too many parameters can lead to your team disagreeing on which to trust or to use to take action. This chapter covers how to create Health Scores that you can trust and how best to take action on the changes to those Health Scores.

The health of your customers has two significant influencers, outcomes and experiences. We discussed the Customer Success equation in Chapter 2.

$$CS = CX + CO$$

For example, you can use a ride-sharing service to get from one place to another. The process of getting from point A to point B is the "outcome" from your ride. How did you feel during the journey? Did you like the music that the driver played? How much of a conversationalist was your driver? Was the route short or the best use of time? That is your "experience."

Both *outcome* and *experience* are equally important to you and will influence your decision to continue using the ride-sharing service at the same frequency or not. If the experience increases in enjoyment, it will most likely increase your use of the service. If the experience continues to be positive, you may advocate the service by recommending it to your friends and colleagues. If the experience changes and becomes unfavorable, the worst-case scenario is that you switch over to a competitor.

The same is true of how your customers work with your product or service. The outcomes and experiences will drive their decision to continue to use your offering, product, or service – or not. In Outcomes Health, the customer must be achieving their outcomes and deriving value for them to be considered healthy. In Experience Health, you must ask, does the customer like the experience of working with our company and product? You need the two Health Score measures, Outcomes and Experience, as indicators of overall customer health.

Designing Your Outcomes Health Score

An Outcomes Health Score helps you track your customers to see if they are achieving their business outcomes and deriving value from your product or service. There are four categories measured by this type of Health Score.

Deployment

Think about an occasion when you purchased and downloaded an app on your phone and registered it for the first time. That is a type of deployment. When tracking a deployment, you measure if the customer has activated the product or service they purchased. The idea is that customers generally subscribe to many things as part of their contract. When they don't activate their purchase, they are not enabled to use your product and won't be able to derive value from it. That leads to churn or cancelling their subscription. That is exactly what you want to avoid.

A typical *deployment* in a Software as a Service (SaaS) business is measured by the number of licenses activated, features enabled, and initial training completed, to name a few. If your product is mostly on-premise, the most common measures will consist of the number of downloads of the software, features or modules enabled, or the first field or services visit.

Engagement

An engagement can be any employee communicating with a customer. It could be Marketing's newest campaign for a new product version, someone from Sales trying to sell them more licenses, or even holding an EBR. Engagement can also refer to a lack of engagement when your customer does not respond or refuses to participate.

An *engagement measurement* tracks how your company is communicating and the level of involvement with the customer's key stakeholders. It helps you identify if communication and engagements are happening regularly. At the very least, you should be in contact with the decision-maker or executive sponsor at your customer on a regular basis. Typically, companies will also want to frequently engage with the power user or administrators of their product or service. More mature companies will also emphasize driving frequent interactions with the end-users of the product. IT organizations can be yet another critical stakeholder, especially in large enterprises. We have even seen companies track event attendance, how many trainings completed, and website visits as useful proxies for human interactions.

Whatever you determine is the best measurement process for your company, you must bear one thing in mind. You cannot afford to manually track your engagement with the important stakeholders at all your customers big and small. It needs to be automated.

Adoption

The term adoption in the tech industry means "product adoption." It refers to the practice of your customers using your product or service. You, the Customer Success Manager, want to ensure the continuous use or adoption of the product. That means you will be responsible for the customer finding value in the product by using it. When measuring *adoption,* you want to track your customers to see if they are using your product as frequently as you would want them to. Adoption can be an indication if your customers are using all the high-value parts of your product or not. You could think of this measure in at least two ways.

The first classification is called the *depth of adoption*. This measurement answers the question "Are users logging in an 'active' way?" Many products and services are deployed in the form of licenses. The most common approach is to measure Daily Active Users, Weekly Active Users, or Monthly Active Users. Depending on the purchase, you should expect your customers to at least use your product in a measured frequency of logins. In some businesses, the volume of activity, transactions, or hours logged in the system is a better measure of the depth of adoption.

If your product is not in the cloud, but more on-premise, there are different measures to consider. The most common include whether your customer has upgraded to the most recent version of your product. Conversely, the metric should show how many versions behind they are. Another proxy signal of usage is the volume of support tickets submitted or the number of training modules completed. You could also track the number of interactions your customers have with your professional services team.

The second classification is the *breadth of adoption*. This type of analysis shows if the full extent of the solution is used healthily. When you break

ILLUSTRATIVE TYPES OF VALUE

Inspirational

*How do we contribute to our customer's
strategic intitiatives and/or values and/or
social responsibility?*

Ease of Doing Business

*How do we add efficiency to our customers?
Do we add expertise to our customers?*

Economic

*Have we improved top line and/or reduced cost
for our customers?*

**Figure 9.1   Illustrative types of business outcomes delivered
to your customers.**

down the usage, you will also see if the right set of features are actively
leveraged. If your company's product has certain features that are especially
"sticky," you will want to ensure that as many of your customers as possible
are taking advantage of that functionality.

Return on Investment (ROI)

An ROI measure tracks whether your customers are achieving the business
outcomes they want from your product or service. If your product can report
how your customers are getting value from your offering, set this score
directly based on that data. If not, companies should create joint success
plans with their customers to track the business outcomes and activities
required to get there. As shown in Figure 9.1, business outcomes or ROI
can be of three illustrative types: economic, ease of doing business, and
inspirational.

Designing Your Experience Health Score

Experience Health Scores help you see if your customer is enjoying their experience working with your company as a vendor or partner. This score involves at least three types of measurements as follows.

Overall Experience

This measure tracks whether the customer's users and stakeholders enjoy working with your company. It even asks and proves if they "like" you enough to be loyal to your company and perhaps advocate on your behalf. Net Promoter Scores (NPS) are a great way to capture this measure.

A Net Promoter Score, or NPS, is a core measurement or method that most companies use to measure overall customer satisfaction. It shows customer health and loyalty. It is also a lead indicator or prediction of future product adoption and growth. Most of you have probably participated in one or two NPS surveys, either online, in an email, or over the phone. The method is to ask a single question: "How likely are you to recommend our product or company to a friend or colleague?" A world-class NPS score is considered anything above 70.

Customer surveys and NPS scores not only measure customer sentiment, they can also indirectly measure your performance as a Customer Success Manager, and the Customer Success program as a whole. Most companies use the NPS score, with other metrics throughout the life of the customer, to gauge overall customer health and success.

Support Experience

You can measure how well support teams are responding to customers' needs by sending a Customer Satisfaction survey after any support engagement. Customers can then rate on a 1–5 scale the question, "How would you rate your overall satisfaction with the service you received?"

- 1: Very unsatisfied
- 2: Unsatisfied
- 3: Neutral
- 4: Satisfied
- 5: Very satisfied.

The results can be averaged out to what is known as a Composite Customer Satisfaction Score or CSAT. The CSAT scores are usually expressed as a percentage scale: 100% being total customer satisfaction and 0% total customer dissatisfaction.

Sentiment Score

As a Customer Success Manager, there will be many data perspectives to consider. It is necessary to gather as much information as you possibly can. That includes looking beyond what the analytic data is telling you. The Sentiment Score measurement tracks the sentiment of the customer's stakeholders as measured by customer-facing employees at your company. It is not just the Customer Success Manager who can attest to the customer's health based on whom they may engage with regularly. Many other people within your organization are connected and communicating with your customer, sometimes not even work-related. For instance, your CS executive may be talking with a corresponding customer's executive. Perhaps your Sales leader may be engaged with one of their critical decision-makers. Each perspective is unique due to their position, their experience, and the type of interaction they have with the customer. Everyone will have a different take on the customer and their overall health.

The Sentiment Score is, at its core, an entirely subjective judgment. It is used to add color and insight to all of your quantitative health data. However, it should never be the only element used to measure health. All must be combined or used in various proportions to present a holistic view of the customer. In truth, the human viewpoint is sometimes the most important of all. When the Sentiment Score is finally gathered, you must capture the results as part of those notes.

Setting the Right Thresholds

For each of the data measurements discussed in this chapter, you will need to determine appropriate thresholds for what is good, average, and bad health. Doing so will help you assess what aspect of your customer's health is at risk or trending poorly and will inform which action you need to take.

For the Outcomes Health Scores, it is recommended to use a minimum of three scores (Red, Yellow, Green) and a maximum of 5 (Red, Orange, Yellow, Light Green, Dark Green) from bad to good. A good practice to decide thresholds is to split your existing customer base into three or five sections, depending on the number of scores that you select. They should be equal groups called tertiles (or quintiles for five groups). Each should be based on a metric, such as the percentage of licenses assigned for deployment. It would be best if you tried to have a balanced view of your customers from the outset. Placing 20% of your customer base in each quintile (or an equal % in each category) will provide more accessible insight as to how well they are performing. It also provides the reference point for growth within your customer base. You should also validate thresholds and related metrics semi-annually/annually to make sure your Health Scores stay relevant. The overall Outcomes Score can be an average of all the underlying measures. You can also choose to weigh specific measures more than others.

For Experience Health Scores, an excellent place to start is with Overall Experience or the Net Promoter Score. As an example, if the NPS for the customer is based on multiple responses with results in the range of 60–100%, you can score the customer green. If the NPS is in the range of 30–60%, you can score the customer yellow. If it's less than 30%, you can score it red. It is similar to your Support Experience scores. If your average rating for the customer is 4 or above, you can score it green. If the score is between 3 and 4, it would be yellow and less than 3 would be red. The Overall Experience score can be an average of all underlying measures. You can also choose to weigh other specific measures more than others.

To calculate the overall score for the customer, take an average of both the Outcomes Score and Experience Score. If you have a hypothesis that one is more important than the other, you can choose to weigh one heavier than the other.

Other Frameworks to Design Your Health Score

While Customer Outcomes and Customer Experience can be genuinely indicative of the health of your customers, there are many other ways to design your Health Scores depending on what you are trying to accomplish with them.

One of the most insightful set of instructions was given in a blog post called "The CEO's Guide to Measuring your Customers," by Nick Mehta, CEO of Gainsight. Nick discussed some approaches to integrating various "signals" from your customers into your Health Scoring that are now becoming a common practice. The emphasis was on the multiple sources of your data. Nick stated that "One of the biggest mistakes companies make when implementing Customer Health Scoring is thinking everything can be distilled down to one number."[1]

Vendor Outcomes Health Score

This score is used if you want to measure the benefit that your customers provide to the growth of your own company (i.e. the vendor). Customers offer multiple areas of value to vendors, and you should measure those areas separately. For a typical vendor, the desired outcomes for you include:

- Value if the client stays with you.
- Incremental value if the client expands with you.
- Incremental value if the client helps you acquire new clients (e.g. as a referral).

A Vendor Outcomes Scorecard could have top-level dimensions of Retention, Expansion, and Advocacy. For Retention, ask: "Are they likely to stay with us?" For Expansion, ask: "Are they likely to expand in spending or consumption with us?" For Advocacy, ask: "Are they likely to be an advocate for us?" Figure 9.2 shows a way to organize this assessment.

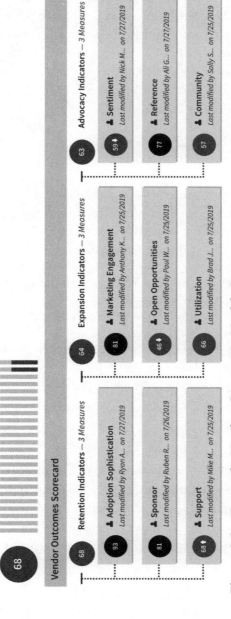

Figure 9.2 Example Vendor Outcomes Health Score.

Vendor Expansion Health Score

Some companies want to easily expose what is known as "white space" for their sales team. The term "white space" refers to the size of the overall opportunity each customer has for greater expansion and recurring revenue. Therefore, your health measures and threshold will be based on your customers' propensity to buy each of the products that you offer. You may find out that it is not always the largest customer that provides the most significant opportunity or "white space."

Customer Engagement Health Score

For many organizations, the focus on customer health is managing "leading indicators." Often, the leading indicators for customer retention and expansion tend to be around the level of engagement between the client and the vendor. A Client Engagement Scorecard might include:

- Product/Service Engagement: How sophisticated is the client's usage of the product/service in question?
- Marketing Engagement: How often does the customer attend webinars, events, etc.?
- Community Engagement: Is the client active in the vendor's online community?
- Advocacy Engagement: Is the client an active advocate for the vendor?

Customer Maturity Health Score

This measure is to be used to calculate your company's efforts to get customers to higher levels of sophistication. Some businesses, particularly with high-touch engagement models, want to drive customers toward increasing levels of maturity with their product. Being able to assess a customer's level of maturity will inform staff and resource assignments to customers based upon that level. A Client Maturity Scorecard could include:

- Business processes: Does the client have business processes implemented around the vendor's product or service?

- Sophistication: How sophisticated is the client's usage of the vendor's product or service?
- Tenure: How long has the client been using the vendor's product or service?
- Training: How many people at the client have been trained on the vendor's product or service?
- Advocacy: Is the client an active advocate for the vendor?

Putting Health Scores to Work for You

When we began to contemplate contributors for this book, we tried to align ourselves with individuals who specialized on both sides of the spectrum of customer success – technology and human beings. We wanted someone who has a strong background in utilizing business interfacing technology while managing people to perform their best. That led us to Erin Siemens. It was her multi-year tenure at ADP that began in Implementation, delivering technology solutions to various sized companies, and her balance as a certified Professional in Human Resources that seemed ideal for our request. Erin spoke at the Pulse 2019 Conference on the subject of deploying customer success across the enterprise and that solidified our choice. We asked Erin to give her view on putting Health Scores into action.

Health Scores in Action

By Erin Siemens, SVP Client Success, ADP

I've been working at making customers successful for a little more than 20 years, and we have always tried to quantify a customer's health. Even now, most organizations' Health Scores usually rely on simple and straightforward ratings like red, yellow, or green. While a lot has changed in 20 years, the determination of what makes a customer's health red, yellow, or green remains in the eye of the beholder. Take, for example, our company's largest manufacturing customer.

(continued)

(continued)

The relationship manager at the time rated the account bright green because she and her customer contact had a fantastic personal relationship. Their kids played on the same high school baseball teams. She had secured him a place in our company's Executive Advisory Board. There was no reason to question the strength or longevity of the business relationship. If we ever had the right to be concerned, we were confident that our loyal customer contact would surely let us know. Eventually, the organization hired a new leader. Our one and only contact's influence waned as the company's direction shifted. Our customer's health rating went from Green to Bright Red overnight with ostensibly no early warning signals. Soon our contact left the company, and the account went radio silent. Before we knew it, we were offboarding the customer to a competitor. It was a painful and costly loss. It was the kind of situation that makes a colleague of mine says, "Green is the color of denial."

There is a need to gauge customer health more effectively. Not just for predicting churn, but so Customer Success Managers can understand the levers they need to pull when there are signs of a struggle in the partnership. These are the five dimensions we've used to measure customer health at my current company, and they should be transferable to any organization.

- Financial health: Is your customer's spend with you increasing or decreasing? Do they have a contract? Are you regularly issuing discounts? Are they paying their bills timely?
- Product utilization: Are you embedded with their strategic functions, or does their organization view you as a commodity/transactional provider?
- Client engagement: Is your customer engaging with you in an advisory capacity to inform your product roadmaps? Do they attend any client events that you host? Are they bothering to provide feedback through your surveys or other means? Are they providing references for your products? Are their executives participating in your partnership meetings?

- Service delivery: Is your customer having a positive experience with your Support teams? Is your support organization delivering to its SLAs and addressing requests in a timely fashion? Is your customer engaging with Support through the right channels? Are they generating an appropriate volume of support requests?
- Churn risk: Has your customer recently had a change in leadership? Are they engaging with competitors? Are they positioning for acquisition?

Once you measure health, you should ensure that you have playbooks that engage the appropriate parts of your organization when you see reduced or poor performance along any of the dimensions. I recommend that you also find a way to share this information with your customers to ensure they understand their role in driving a healthy partnership and actively take part in improving their outcomes.

Just as the Customer Success industry continues to evolve and learn from these relatively new disciplines, my perspective on what's essential in measuring customer health continues to change. Some adjustments we'll make to my current company's Health Score will include measuring a customer's progress in achieving their desired outcomes and measuring health across the individual products a customer uses with us. As you implement and adopt a Health Score for your organization, you will quickly see the opportunities for you to adjust and evolve your methodology as well.

My parting advice to anyone beginning this journey is to get the process moving. Do not wait until you think you have the perfect approach. Use the data you have and design your Health Score around it. You will never have complete data. The funny thing about data is that it only starts to get better when people start using it. Ensure that your customer health information is visible across your organization; from Product to Technical Support to Sales. Use Health Scores to make decisions that are driven by and for your customers and their success. Your Health Score data will not be perfect. It will be something that continues to evolve and change as you learn more. Your customers, however, and your organization will benefit immediately from the first steps to measuring and acting to improve customer health in an intentional and data-driven way.

As Erin Siemens shared, there must be multi-sourced data that you use to develop your scorecards. That, however, is not enough. The customer health information gained will amount to nothing if it is not utilized properly. It must be visible for all customer-facing employees so that they may act on that information accordingly. Most of all, don't allow your lack of data to scare you into complacency. That is just denial and ultimately cowardly. Being proactive to gain more data and move to help customers attain their goals lead to what customer success is: putting customers first.

The Future and Human-Element of Customer Health Scorecards

Our world is increasingly able to use incredible amounts of data. With the rapid advancement in Data Science and Artificial Intelligence, you may wonder what role do human beings play in the present and future of Customer Success Managers?

Normalization vs. Individualization

Health Scores by design normalize and minimize customer uniqueness. Think about that for a moment. The model typically applies a broad set of health criteria and predetermined thresholds across a large collection of customers. It doesn't take into account the unique qualities of every customer. Instead, Health Scores serve the purpose of surfacing much-needed intelligence on how all your customers are doing by applying customer health models. We know, however, there is a growing undercurrent. On the surface, the exercise of health scoring, which essentially rationalizes-out the uniqueness of each customer into categories may seem to contradict an increasing expectation from customers that they should receive a more customized experience.

If you consider the concept of segmentation and grouping customers together based on similarities, like revenue, industry, product mix, maturity level, along with customer health scoring, the formulaic approach further mutes the uniqueness of each customer. So, we run the risk of not addressing the reality that customers must be as different from each other as any person is from the next.

To explain the uniqueness of your customers, let's use an analogy of parenting. Imagine a couple raising three children. As a new parent, you first try to apply the same parenting "playbooks" you learned in your upbringing. Maybe you were one of those more progressive parents who read a few books or attended seminars to improve your parenting skills. Nonetheless, despite your best efforts, that poor first child of yours was the de facto guinea pig. With the first-born, you likely learned more about what didn't work than what did. As a result, you learned to develop more mature playbooks and began to build a virtual Health Score with better indicators that led to certain behaviors. Your parental "Spidey-sense" becomes keener over time. However, every child that follows requires a different version of your playbooks. The same playbooks never work uniformly across all children. A similar parallel can be made for every new customer that comes into your own managed portfolio. You can try the same old plays for your new customers, but at some point along their journey, you will have to adjust your approach.

Whether you are coaching a child or a customer, the human factor demands a distinctive stratagem to serve the unique needs of each. Overlooking a customer's unique needs is the fundamental flaw of current health scoring and segmentation models. While scorecards give you a decent perspective on health, they don't tell the whole story, nor do they maximize each customer's potential.

The deficiency of a "scorecard only" system is why the Customer Success Manager in an organization is so incredibly vital. By interacting directly with the individual customer when possible, the Customer Success Manager catalyzes the success of the customer and continuously adds value to an ongoing relationship with the solution provider. The CEO, leveraging the same customer Health Score model as the Customer Success Manager, uses aggregated health data to make broad determinations across the entire customer base and assess how customer segments are trending directionally. However, they do not typically have the time to examine each and every customer. The Customer Success Manager, on the other hand, is holistically responsible for every customer in their book of business. The Customer Success Manager helps to tailor and serve their individual customers' needs while applying a generalized playbook. So, we have a gap of sorts: Health Score models that serve to generalize and customers that expect customization.

Artificial Intelligence vs. Emotional Intelligence

The human Customer Success Manager helps to factor the variable of the customer's individuality back into the Health Score formula. The CSM often does so in real-time through a customized approach best-suited for each customer. It's notable that "customized" and "customer" share the same root word from the Latin word *consuetudinem* meaning "habit, usage, way, practice, tradition, familiarity."[2] Everyone has habits, practices, and traditions that are unique to them. Sometimes there is a need for awareness to recognize the uniqueness. The point is that there are real people associated with each customer score and groups of real people associated with each of the segments you have established.

Advancements are coming in Artificial Intelligence that will enable a CS platform to account for AI-interpreted facial expressions and vocal tone emotion patterns in real-time. It will "assess" the customer sentiment during a live video call. However, the Customer Success Manager today is providing an invaluable and still much needed customized approach to customer engagement. What needs to be discussed is the idea of prediction vs. judgment. This was the topic of an interesting interview by Karen Christensen of Rotman Magazine with the Chief Economist of the Creative Destruction Lab and author, Joshua Gans. The title of the article and case study was "Prediction vs. Judgment."[3]

Gans quickly outlined the definition of prediction. He stated that "Prediction occurs when you use information that you have to produce information that you do not have . . . Importantly, this is all machine learning does. It does not establish causal relationships and it must be used with care in the face of uncertainty and limited data." For us, this is an indicator that two things must happen in the partnership between humans and AI. First, there must be multi-sourced data. Second, there is always a place for judgment on behalf of human beings. Gans echoed this when he stated, "*People needn't worry:* Artificial intelligence is <u>not</u> about replacing human cognition. As indicated, AI really only 'does' one aspect of intelligence, and that is prediction. The complexity of AI lies in its algorithmic coding, not so much in its results."

Gans surmised that while AI gives us the understanding by formulating predictions through the interpretation of vast amounts of data, AI is "always restricted by what it knows" or rather what it doesn't. Gans went on to state that nothing can replace the three types of human "data": what we receive through our senses, what we control via our preferences, and what we do out of concern for privacy. The power of our senses surpasses that of any machine. A machine can only tell us about *what* our preferences are, they cannot choose them for us. The last form of human "data" was extremely enlightening. Machines can only make predictions based on the information given. Gans explained that "For as long as enough people keep their financial situations, health status and thoughts to themselves, the prediction machines will have insufficient data to predict many types of behavior. As such, our understanding of other humans will always demand judgment skills that machines cannot learn." Ultimately, nothing can replace sound human judgment.

This does not diminish the need for gaining insight through health scoring by any means. We must appreciate what AI can do. However, we must recognize what AI cannot do. There are current level-set limitations of modeling your customers that can only be accomplished by human judgment and personal engagement.

There is a new term that is applicable here called micro-segmentation. It is the small but numerous variations that on their own are not significant but in aggregate can make one customer as unique as the next. Micro-segmentation will probably be the future state of customer intelligence systems, health scoring, and segmentation models. In the meantime, you may have a set of customers with very similar ARR, similar in size, sharing a related industry, situated in similar geographic regions, and so forth. These similar customers may also have equivalent Health Score metrics. While these segmented customers may appear to be practically the same based on current modeling techniques, customers will eventually require different approaches based on elements not tracked or discerned by your Health Score. That approach is the human factor.

Consider that most people are already micro-segmentation experts. It's your natural ability to read people in real-time and discern what approach works best for Person A vs. Person B. All of that delineating data is being assessed, processed, and logged in your brain. In essence, micro-segmentation allows for a system, in this case, a human being, to efficiently sift through that incredibly long list of variables unique to each human customer that you interact with in real-time. It's a skill today that humans do better at processing than software. Until we cross that threshold, and perhaps even after, Customer Success Managers hold a vital role in de-normalizing Health Scores and re-constituting the unique elements of each customer so that when taking actions, they are delivered in a manner tailored uniquely to them.

In the end, as a Customer Success practitioner, the thing that you will draw the most value and reward from is human interaction. For the foreseeable future, as long as humans are buying and using products we serve up, Customer Success Managers will be needed as scorecard interpreters and injectors of sincere actions. This human interaction will ensure that each customer attains as personalized an experience as is humanly possible.

●●●

As was described earlier in this chapter, your success as a Customer Success Manager is critically tied to how well you design and implement scorecards. Your customer's scorecards aren't a panacea or a one-size fits all prevention of churn. It is absolutely necessary, however, to utilize the information to advance your company's growth. You should be on the lookout for an amazing ride into the future when it comes to measuring customer health and serving up customized engagement through an evolving Customer Success approach.

Endnotes

1. Mehta, N., Srinivasan, P., and Robins, W. (2018). Measuring Your Customers. [Gainsight.com]. 24 July 2018. Retrieved from: https://www.gainsight.com/blog/ceos-guide-measuring-customers/.
2. Online Etymology Dictionary. (c) 2001-2009. Douglas Harper. Retrieved from https://www.etymonline.com/search?q=consuetudinem
3. Gans, J. and Christensen, K. (2019). Exploring the impact of artificial intelligence: prediction vs. judgment. *Rotman Magazine* (1 January 2019).

10

Voice of the Customer and Your Tech-Touch Strategy

In the previous chapter, we discussed Health Scores as a diagnostic tool to help you manage your customers more effectively by knowing if they are achieving their outcomes and desired experiences. In this chapter, we'll cover how to effectively listen to your customers' feedback and act on it. We'll also talk about your tech-touch strategy, scaling your processes using email automation and in-product engagements, so you can reach more customers without human intervention.

How to Get Meaningful Customer Feedback

A couple of decades ago, Business to Business (B2B) companies were not actively surveying their customers to get their feedback first hand. Over time, surveying methods improved dramatically. You could now argue that companies are guilty of over surveying their customers. Nonetheless, what are they doing with the data? At this point, companies face the challenge of having the data but still not having a consistent and closed-loop approach to improving customer experience. We often observe that not all customers have the right opportunities to offer feedback, or that feedback doesn't get acted on or escalated reliably. When follow-up does occur, we do not have visibility into whether it was effective.

There is a great need to make the process of getting customer feedback and closing the loop with your customers more consistent and predictable. To accomplish this, we recommend a four-step method of identifying and acting on customer experience feedback.

- **Listen to the customer:** there is only one way to capture the types of data that provide perspectives on the customer's experience, and that is by listening to the customer.
- **Capture the voice of the customer:** act on customer signals in real-time and be sure all "Voice of the Customer" feedback programs include a closed-loop response and action plan.
- **Raise the visibility of progress:** analyze the progress against customer experience. This analysis provides visibility to management, teams, and Customer Success Managers.
- **Receive input across the organization:** improve the customer experience based on input from relevant departments.

Listen to the Customer

The first step in attaining customer feedback is soliciting it and then listening to your customers. As described earlier, a highly recommended listening method would be NPS surveys. The surveys should be sent out every six months to every customer. Decision-makers typically tend to respond better to email surveys while end-users respond better to surveys triggered by your product or in-product because it is more timely and contextual. For Support Customer Satisfaction (CSAT) surveys, they should be sent right after a major interaction or when a support case is completed.

Acknowledge the Feedback

Once you have heard the customer's feedback, it is vital to act on it. For your higher-value customers, it's essential to reach out manually and acknowledge their input. You need to leverage more automation for your smaller

Thank you for your survey response

Hi Alex,

Thank you for taking the time to share your feedback. It sounds like there could be some opportunities to improve your experience with Gainsight.

I'm so happy to see that you'd recommend Gainsight. We work hard every day to improve the product and support every customer. Your positive rating means Gainsight is headed in the right direction.

I want to understand what's working well with Gainsight and where we can still improve. I will add this as an action item for our next meeting. If there is something pressing, please let me know.

Sincerely,

Figure 10.1   Example of a closed loop email follow-up for a Promoter NPS Response.

customers. If you're responding to a Promoter NPS feedback, send a thank you email with a request for them to participate in your customer reference program. Recall that your Promoters are your most significant source for customer advocates. Another option is an online advocacy program, such as G2 Crowd or TrustRadius. Figure 10.1 is an example of a simple email template to thank Promoters for their survey responses. Figure 10.2 is an example of an email template to request participation in an advocacy program.

Thank you for your survey response

Hi Sarah,

Thank you for your high score! You honestly made my day! If you have a few minutes, would you be willing to write a quick review to make it easier for other people to discover Gainsight?

Share your Gainsight experience

Sincerely,

Figure 10.2   Example of a closed loop email follow-up to elicit advocacy.

If you are following up on a Passive NPS response, send a thank you email with a request for a follow-up call to learn more details. If appropriate, you could include links to blog posts or newsletters on product usage as suggestions. Following up on a Detractor NPS response warrants a quick response. First, send a follow-up email recognizing their feedback. Inquire about their answers, respectfully probing for more information. Lastly, request a call or an in-person meeting, if applicable. You may choose to engage the Executive Sponsor at your end, especially for higher-value customers.

Analyze the Information

Now that you've collected feedback and followed up for more details, you have a treasure trove of information. It would help if you used this time to analyze the data and turn it into insights that your company can use to become more customer-centric. Many platforms provide text analytics capability to find common trends and words used in survey responses. You can look for mentions related to product and features, services (e.g. Support, Customer Success), and value delivered (see Figure 10.3). It is also important to see trends over time. Look for improvements or declines after milestone events, such as product releases or user training sessions.

Figure 10.3   Example of word clouds and text analytics based on survey responses.

Implement Results of the Analysis

Finally, use the insights to improve individual functions within your company or increase cross-functional collaboration to become more customer-centric as a company. As a Customer Success Manager, you have the privilege and responsibility of sharing these insights with the company as the voice of your customer. If there is a pattern within customer responses, share it with the departments or teams, and make relevant changes. For example, if a poor user interface is a common reason for low NPS, share the findings with the Product team. If the onboarding process is complicated and a common cause for low NPS, redesign the onboarding process. You can also create case studies to share with the broader company, especially if there is a correlation between NPS and company performance.

The Hidden Value of Customer Feedback

As we began to formulate the different chapters and their topics in this book, we came to the subject of the customer's voice and tech touch. What is intriguing is that tech touch often seems like a voiceless segment due to all the automation and non-personal outreaches. It is actually anything but that. We approached Stephanie Berner, who is the current Global Head of Customer Success at LinkedIn Sales Solutions, to share her views on the issue of getting meaningful feedback from your customers, especially from those who are primarily tech touch. She submitted a simple, yet profound story about "Prospecting for Gold."

Prospecting for Gold

by Stephanie Berner, Global Head of Customer Success at LinkedIn Sales Solutions

Shortly after rolling out our customer survey program, I announced to my team a new training curriculum to build skills in prospecting. In shock, the team clearly objected to any implication that they would be

(continued)

(*continued*)

doing the job of the sales team. "How is this at all relevant to customer feedback?" they groaned. Despite their disagreement, I proceeded.

I told them the story of the gold miners of the mid-1800s. Soon after gold nuggets were discovered in the American River in 1848, crowds flooded the Sacramento Valley. They dove head-first, so to speak, into panning for gold nuggets in the pebbles at the bottom of the river. Many got a little lucky this way, but they were looking for the obvious nuggets in plain sight. None, however, made it big. A select few opted for a different method. They sought clues in the water flow, surrounding geology, and even the vegetation. These genius prospectors discovered that certain patterns hinted at the mother lode under the surface. These were the prospectors who struck it rich.

The genius in customer feedback is not individual data points like survey scores, individual comments, the presence or absence of a response. It is found in the insight that emerges when we look at the surrounding clues. A low relationship score and a positive comment about a particular feature could hint at unrealized value. Low stakeholder sentiment alongside high end-user sentiment signals a need for stronger stakeholder engagement, while the opposite signals latent risk. Consistent response from a program administrator and an unexpected response from a new executive provides an open door to start a new conversation about return on investment.

The clues lead to patterns, the patterns lead to insight, the insight leads to action. When taken across a collection of customers, even your tech-touch customers, these nuggets unfold into a mother lode of information and insights. They have endless applicability across the business: product, churn forecasting, stakeholder engagement, emerging opportunities, and more. A single conversation or an email that follows up on the pattern of feedback can change the trajectory of any customer relationship.

"Customer feedback is like gold nuggets," I told my team. "Each data point is useful, yes, but we strike it rich when we really go hunting for the mother lode. Don't stop at the score, whether high *or* low. Be those genius gold prospectors and look for clues that lead to patterns in order to understand what's really going on." I continued with a few examples of Customer Success Managers finding their "golden nugget" to bring this concept to life for them.

Jody's customer was unresponsive, but not unhealthy. With decent product adoption, strong end-user product feedback, near-zero technical issues, and a history of straightforward, flat renewals, it was tempting for Jody to assume everything was fine. So, she spent her time with other, more problematic customers. The one problem nagging at Jody? It was nearly impossible to get the customer to do a QBR, let alone take a phone call. She had nearly given up when her program administrator replied to the bi-annual relationship survey with a Likelihood to Recommend score of 9. Digging further, Jody discovered a *nugget* in the comments section: the customer liked the product but noticed that competitive products seemed to be innovating faster with new use-cases.

As you can imagine, Jody sprang into action, using the survey response as a "reason" to engage and educate the customer on recent product innovation and new use-cases. Together, they developed a refreshed success plan that leveraged already-positive adoption trends to help users engage in new use-cases and lean on new functionality. If Jody had simply stopped at the initial data – positive adoption, no red flags, good survey score – she would have missed the underlying signal of latent risk. Within six weeks the customer not only committed to renewal but started conversations for a 100% increase in spend.

Kevin was a Customer Success Manager who took the customer relationship survey seriously. The relationship survey launched while one of his team members was on vacation. Kevin stepped in and diligently watched his Customer Success Manager's survey responses closely and closed the loop with every high-value customer. In one case, the score came in at 7, with the comment: "We are happy enough, but it's just too expensive." Kevin dug into the situation further and found the customer continued to grow organically year-on-year, without any volume discounts. After engaging with the Account Executive to arrive at a pricing structure that would allow the customer to grow at a more sustainable pace, Kevin led the conversation with the customer to help them understand how a lower seat price, but longer commitment, would ultimately deliver more value and stronger outcomes.

(continued)

(continued)

Haley was an enterprise Customer Success Manager. She found an interesting mismatch in the feedback data that she turned into an opportunity. The relationship/decision-maker NPS was consistently passive. The main points of contact were reluctant to commit to ongoing user education and training on the product. This limited use-case development and kept their program from advancing. Prospecting for information, Haley successfully accessed the end-user product NPS data for this customer. She found a mother lode! The end-user NPS was consistently high. The users raved about the value. They also asked for more training to be able to do more with the product and potentially retire other, less useful technologies in parallel. In the next QBR, Haley showcased the strong end-user NPS as part of the ROI story. More importantly, she pulled direct end-user quotes to showcase the demand for more consistent training and education. The customer agreed to a new success plan centered around training and new use-case development. This fully mitigated a latent churn risk and changed the trajectory of the relationship. What's more, Haley used this story to showcase to the Product team the importance of sharing end-user NPS data with Customer Success Managers.

After Stephanie shared these stories with us, we understood why her team was so inspired to look for "golden nuggets" of their own. This is just an illustration of how, as a Customer Success Professional, you can never stop listening to the voice of the customer. You might have to dig a little bit and find the feedback in remote places, but if you do, you have an opportunity to turn it into the real treasure of success.

Tech Touch: The Secrets of Low-Touch Customer Success

Earlier in the book, the subject of "segmentation" was discussed. One segment that was not addressed was that of "low-touch" or "tech-touch" customers. Most companies generally have a "long tail" of smaller customers with low revenue per customer. The term "long tail" was initially used by the former editor of *Wired magazine,* Chris Anderson. He introduced the business concept both in articles and his 2006 book *The Long Tail: Why the Future of Business Is Selling Less of More.*[1] The long tail concept is that the total volume of less popular goods that are not in high demand can increase profits overall. In the SaaS industry and the field of Customer Success, the "long tail" applies to your smaller customers that when thought of as a combined entity can be a large and profitable business. They might not have the high visibility of enterprise clients, but they also don't have the demands that can eat away profitability. Over time, you will find that tech-touch customers have staying power and the ability to make money in aggregate.

It's hard to serve tech-touch customers economically by staffing Customer Success Managers in this segment. If your business is blessed with high margins even in this segment, the most common themes you are likely to hear include "My Customer Success Managers are overworked" or "Our Customer Success Managers spend a lot of time on repetitive activities" or "We have so many Small-to-Medium Business (SMB) customers that our Customer Success Managers cannot effectively reach out to all of them at a regular cadence." If any of these sounds familiar, you need a Tech Touch strategy to complement your Customer Success Managers.

It's important to address that having a large segment of tech-touch clients doesn't mean you relinquish the role of the Customer Success Manager. The purpose of the Customer Success Manager is very critical. Tech touch means you are starting with automation and digital engagement to get more scale and involving a human being only when required. When implemented right, your tech-touch strategy aims to automate processes to efficiently manage your long-tail customers across their lifecycle. The idea is to surface risks and expansion opportunities across a large segment of customers with the ultimate goal of prioritizing human intervention only for the most critical situations. In this section, we will discuss the most commonly used use-cases for tech-touch programs.

Onboarding Tech-Touch Workflow

Companies with products that are relatively easy to set up or where the customer's boarding can be measured in days rather than weeks or months should carefully consider a tech-touch strategy for their onboarding workflow. There are some steps to assist you as you consider which onboarding workflow works best for your company and your customers (Figure 10.4).

- After a prospect signs the contract and becomes a customer, it's important to reach out to them within a day or two to welcome them, present what they should expect over the next few days, and what is required from them. You could use an email outreach to start this process.

- Engagement at these early days is critical because you have the momentum and buzz of starting a relationship. Make the most of the early days. If your customer doesn't open the email and click on any of the links that you've highlighted, you should consider it a risk and have a human being reach out to course-correct immediately. Progress in the early days sets the tone for the rest of the relationship.

- After a couple of days, send an email with the first training courses to get an introduction to the product or service. Also, include any links to your technical support process. For example, phone numbers or a link to a support website in case there are any technical challenges.

- If the customer continues as planned, wait a few more days before contacting them. Then send them another email outlining installation instructions – something where they can download and click next to configure.

- If the configuration was successful and the customer starts using the product, send them some tips and tricks to start using the basic functions. You can use either the email channel or in-product pop-up messages to convey the same.

- Send them a congratulatory message when they are "live" on your product and are actively using it for a week or two. If at any point the customer doesn't complete any of the onboarding processes, try sending reminders and, if that doesn't work, have a human being intervene and talk to the customer to bring them back on track.

- Finally, close out with a Customer Satisfaction survey delivered by email or in-product to better understand if the experience along the journey was to their satisfaction. As you know, there's much you can learn from these surveys.

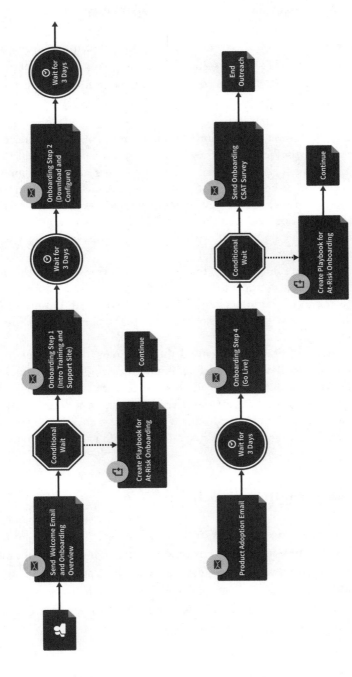

Figure 10.4   An example of an onboarding tech-touch workflow.

Renewals Management Tech–Touch Workflow

Another important workflow for companies with subscription revenues is the renewals workflow. Here are some steps to help you think through the renewals workflow for your company to implement for your customers (Figure 10.5).

- About 90–120 days before any customer's renewal, you should reach out to them and make sure they know about the upcoming milestone. You could use emails triggered at that time or use in-product communications. Some companies also choose to ask a one-question survey in that same email about the customer's likelihood to renew. An example would be "At this point in time, how likely are you to renew the subscription with Company X" with the options being Not Likely, Unsure, Likely to Renew, as an example
- If the customer doesn't open the email or doesn't respond to the question, you should consider the customer a "risk" and have a human being reach out. If the customer responds to the survey with Unsure or Not Likely to renew, have a Customer Success Manager reach out to the customer
- It's also a best practice to remind the customer 60 days prior to the renewal by email or in-product communications. Some companies also incentivize customers (especially the ones that are "Unsure") with discounts, tickets to events, free services, or training to sign early renewals
- Finally, after the customer signs the renewal, automate a thank you email to the customer for their business and continued partnership

Risk Management Tech–Touch Workflow

Proactively managing customer risks is a fundamental activity of a Customer Success Manager. For your smaller customers, using tech touch to get more scale is a critical workflow for most companies. A typical use-case is when usage of your product or service drops significantly or logins have stopped in the past few days, as an example. Here are a few guidelines to keep in mind working with tech touch (Figure 10.6):

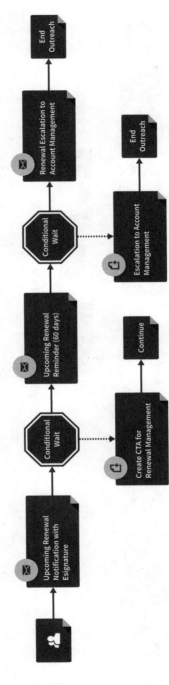

Figure 10.5 An example of a renewals management tech-touch workflow.

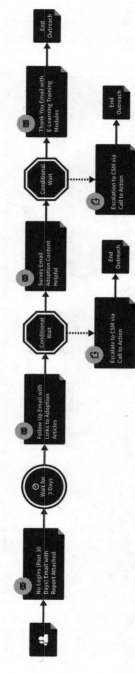

Figure 10.6 An example of a risk management tech-touch workflow.

- Every 30 days, evaluate which customers have dropped in the usage of your product or service and send them a report of the change in adoption with an option for them to talk to their Customer Success Manager.
- After waiting for a few days, follow-up with some case studies or ideas for improving adoption. You could also use recent product release notes to provide new value-added tips for users to log back into the system.
- If adoption improves, survey the customer by email or in-product engagement to check which of the adoption content they found useful. This will help further promote the most useful content going forward.
- If the emails are going unread or usage hasn't picked up in the next couple of weeks, have the Customer Success Manager call the customer.

Advocacy Management Tech–Touch Workflow

Once your customers are finding value in your product, it's an excellent opportunity for the CSM to request the customer to be an advocate for your company. For your smaller customers, it's wise to use tech touch to get more scale in your advocacy workflow. A typical use–case is requesting the customer to be an advocate for you when they respond to an NPS or Customer Satisfaction survey agreeing to be a Promoter for your company (Figure 10.7).

- Automate the sending of the survey either by email or by in–product notifications. You can also send reminders if the customer has opened the email but not responded, or if the customer has partially completed the survey but hasn't submitted the response.
- If the customer responds negatively to the survey, alert the Customer Success Manager to follow-up for more details.
- If the customer responds positively to the survey, you can send another email or in-product notification to check if they would be willing to be an advocate for you. Some companies also send small gift cards or other tokens of appreciation for completing the survey and agreeing to be an advocate.

•••

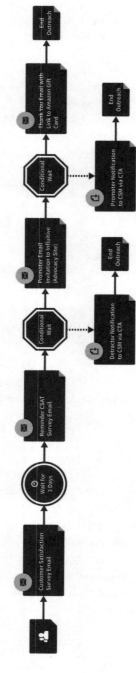

Figure 10.7 An example of an advocacy management tech–touch workflow.

This chapter should have hopefully given you some templates and processes to close the loop with your customers who have given you valuable feedback about their experiences with your product and company. It's a treasure trove of information that you can analyze to take your company to the next level. You should also be able to strategically use digital journeys to reach your customers at scale. As we move forward to the next chapters, we will dive into some other key Customer Success processes.

Endnote

1. Anderson, C. (2006). *The Long Tail*. New York, NY: Hyperion Publishing.

11

Help Customers Achieve Their Business Goals

Helping your customers achieve their business goals is the pinnacle of your job as a Customer Success Manager. The desire alone won't get you there. You must be action-oriented and work collaboratively with your customers on setting up specific plans for their success. Your plans have to include mutually agreed on milestones and data indicators to measure success objectively. Next, through active monitoring, you will help them adopt the use of your product, and coach them through any change management challenges they encounter.

Of course, without a great product, adoption will be far more difficult. It will be imperative, therefore, to have a discerning awareness of your customers' sentiment and practical use of your product, where they might be struggling, what they love about it, and what they dislike. As a result, you should find yourself aligned with your own company's product team as you advocate for a better product for your current and future customers.

Finally, you will need to make sure customers are educated accordingly on proper and best-practice use. All too often, however, customer-facing content, education, and collateral materials are disparate and not well coordinated across your own company, making it challenging to get the best information into the hands of the customer that meets their specific situation: the right message to the right customer at the right time. We will cover all these topics herein.

Adoption Management: How to Proactively Manage Product Use and Adoption

Adoption management or the term "adoption" refers to the process of customers using your product in the most optimal way it was intended to be used. It is typically measured by the total number of people using it, the frequency, and the degree of available features being utilized. Usually, it starts as part of the go-live or shortly after implementation but is more influenced and governed by how well your customer handles the change management required for widespread use. In other words, humans are creatures of habit and introducing your product to their workflow is a disruption and change. Sometimes the change is welcomed. Sometimes is it met with resistance.

Customer Success Managers are predominantly responsible for improving adoption. The idea here is to get customers actively using your products. Have they woven its use into their daily operations and procedures? Are they attaining expected value? If so, the likelihood of them renewing is far more significant, and that can naturally extend into opportunities for expansion. Undoubtedly, as we learned from the same benchmark survey referenced in Chapter 2 (Figure 2.1), there is a good reason why "improving product adoption" is a top 3 priority for Customer Success teams.

Interestingly, adoption management is handled differently at nearly every company. Still, we hear a common set of concerns:

- We don't have clear visibility into which customers are struggling with adoption.
- Our response is inconsistent even when we can identify a customer's adoption level is improving or declining.
- Our interventions are far too time-consuming with unpredictable efficacy.

- Key customer stakeholders (e.g. managers of Customer Success teams or power users) do not have adoption information at their disposal and therefore can't manage their teams' adoption challenges in real-time.

Companies of every type need a standard best practice adoption framework that can provide the following:

- Identify, diagnose, and quickly prioritize customers under-utilizing your product.
- Deliver consistent and scalable interventions through automated outreaches and standardized playbooks.
- Understand which approaches are making the largest impact on improving adoption and operationalize the lessons.

Figure 11.1 illustrates a virtuous cycle of adoption management, whereby you must first identify what the measures of "adoption" mean for your product. Next, prioritize which customers require intervention, and take appropriate human-led or digital-led action. Then, refine your tracking and prioritization thresholds based on lessons learned. Rinse and repeat.

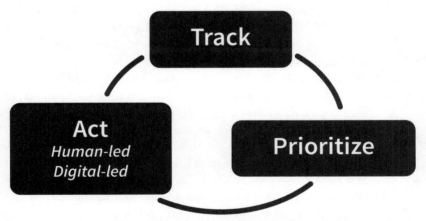

Figure 11.1   Adoption management cycle: track, prioritize, and act.

When operationalizing your approach, there are four essential areas you need to consider in order to be successful at improving the customer's adoption of your product:

1. Establish a standard method of what healthy versus unhealthy adoption looks like across all your customers, by segment. See Chapter 9 on Health Scores.

2. Design standard scripts, or what is commonly referred to as a "playbook," that details the steps you should take under various adoption circumstances. Here are some additional ideas for you to consider:

   - **Deployment review:** investigate opportunities to get your customers to start activating licenses, enabling features, completing initial training, downloading the software, completing the first field or services visit. If they don't start using your product or service, they cannot adopt it healthily. The typical playbook starts with checking with your Sales or Onboarding teams about the intended use for the undeployed licenses or features. Then, reach out to your Executive Sponsors at the customer and co-create an action plan to alleviate the problem.

   - **Chairsides:** shadow end users to determine knowledge and usage gaps. Sit with people who use your product to observe how they run their day. A chairside can be done virtually or in-person. Use the opportunity to determine their level of knowledge of your product or identify usage gaps. You can then better recommend changes to improve overall workflow efficiency and effectiveness and associated training programs.

   - **Instance optimization:** evaluate your customer's product configuration and recommend changes to better match their needs (usually after conducting a chairside). This process can help alleviate "technical debt" – a concept in software development that reflects the implied cost of additional rework caused by choosing an easy or limited solution now instead of using a better approach that would take longer.

   - **Adoption review:** closely examine how your customer's best users are leveraging your product. Identify patterns on what they might be doing differently than others and try to understand why.

   - **Office hours with end-users:** schedule a regular time for your customer's users to ask any questions about usability or provide ad hoc feedback.

- **Feature rollouts:** promote new releases, especially if they solve long-standing issues or challenges your customer may be having. Highlight user-experience improvements such as fewer clicks.
- **Training refresh:** provide a training refresher, especially if adoption stalled during the original implementation and it has been several months since.
- **Best practice guidance:** discuss change management challenges. Also, share with your customer stakeholders what other customers are doing to promote better use of your product and the business impact it is having. In some cases, it would be wise to introduce your customer to other customers who are healthier in their adoption of your product or service.
- **Product–use nurture campaign:** use a drip campaign organized around a theme or feature that is not being leveraged, even by your healthy customers.

3. Determine which customers need attention. Ultimately, you won't be able to do this well at scale. You will need technology to help surface the customers needing the most attention based on criteria and notification thresholds that you set. A couple of simple dashboards can bring a significant improvement in your capacity to intervene for the right customer at the right time. Figure 11.2 shows a heatmap of all customers managed by a Customer Success Manager, and which metrics in the Health Score are the problem areas. If you see that the Deployment score is red, you can run deployment reviews; if the Adoption score is red, you can prioritize adoption and instance reviews. Figure 11.3 is a weekly trend of key health metrics – this shows you if your actions (e.g. deployment reviews, adoption reviews) are achieving their outcome of improving deployment and adoption scores.

4. Share adoption information with your customers. Your customer stakeholders need to know whether they're getting value from their purchase and how to get even more. A key indicator of value is whether or not your product is being used. More importantly, it is ultimately up to your customer to be the internal champion at their company because you can't unilaterally solve adoption issues for your client. Providing them with adoption data will help you to align accordingly. To get scale, share adoption information by email with your sponsors at your customers every week (Figure 11.4 shows an email template to share adoption information).

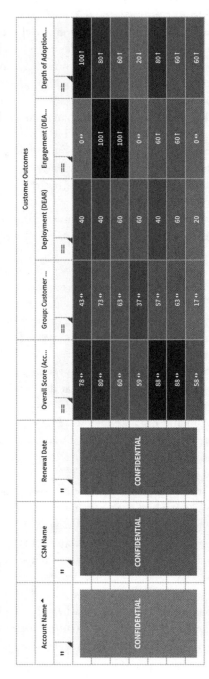

Figure 11.2 Simple view of accounts managed by a specific Customer Success Manager, which includes Customer Deployment and Adoption scores.

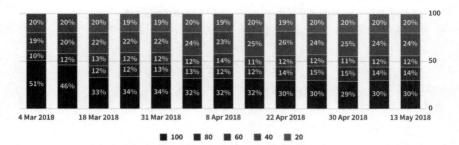

Figure 11.3   Weekly trend of Deployment and Adoption health in a Customer Success Manager portfolio of managed customers.

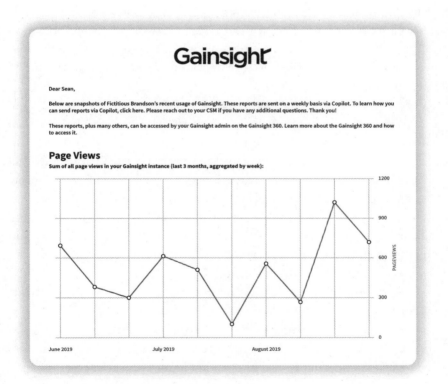

Figure 11.4   Email template to share adoption information with your customers.

Success Planning: Make Sure the Customer Gets the Long-Term Results They Expect

Success planning is the process of the vendor and the customer mutually agreeing to common goals of the partnership, including the tactical steps required to achieve the goals, key milestones to measure success along the way, and timelines associated with achieving the goals. It serves to promote joint accountability to the goals set forth, typically at the beginning of your engagement with them, but not limited to new customers. It should ultimately answer this question with precision: "What are the specific things we must achieve and how will we know we've done so, to secure your renewal year after year?"

There will be times, however, that you'll need to create impromptu plans that focus more on shorter-term objectives. Such strategies include get-well plans for customers at risk to align cross-functional collaboration to drive success for a customer, advocacy plans to push the customer into being a full-fledged "promoter" of your product and company, and for ad hoc targeting of customer goals.

Begin by identifying which customers and which segments you want to bolster with a formal Success Plan. Determine if they will be preserved for your most strategic customers, and thereby customized for each one, or if you plan to standardize them across similar customers. Consider starting with a small subset of customers. You'll need to get comfortable with crafting and maintaining Success Plans. You will, of course, need to establish a consistent process that can be repeated as you fan out to include more customers in Success Planning. The process must consist of three main ingredients: find out the customer's business objectives, identify the actions required to attain those objectives, and then take action as planned.

We recommend a simple and universal framework, like ours, for creating Success Plans. The phases and related steps are self-evident. However, it is important to note that Success Plans are not static. Customer Success Plans are not set-it-and-forget-it artifacts. They are dynamic and require curation and regular attention. It is, as illustrated in Figure 11.5, an ongoing process. If you are making rapid progress and complete Success Plans to deliver value, you will need to work with the customer to plan the next set of goals. Your customers' business objectives may change with respect to priorities. For

Figure 11.5 Success Plan process.

example, your customer may acquire another company and integrating that company now supersedes all goals previously discussed. Maybe the goals set forth at the beginning of the year were too ambitious, and you need to reset expectations on timing as you execute on the plan. All of these are reasons why Customer Success Plans are dynamic and require constant iterations.

Identify Business Objectives

To identify business objectives, conduct the conversation during the initial new customer "Welcome" Moment of Truth. Your goal is to build a deep understanding beyond what the Sales team identified and presumably shared with you during their discovery process. Be prepared to cover this for more than one meeting. Consider the various stakeholders, both laterally and vertically within the customer organization that may have vital information to give. Also, establish appropriate expectations with the desired persons you would like input from in advance of your planning conversation. Be sure to establish both qualitative and quantitative measures of success (Table 11.1).

Strategy Session

The purpose of a strategy session is first to attain stakeholder agreement from the customer about their business objectives. You will also learn the specific challenges that need to be addressed with the help of your products and services. Start by sharing your recommendation or proven best practices,

Table 11.1   Quantitative and qualitative success measures and related pitfalls.

Identify Business Objectives	Pitfalls: Customer Stated Goals
Quantitative: - 10% increase in gross retention in the next fiscal year - 90% of onboardings under 30 days - 10% decrease in escalations from customers in their first 3 months **Qualitative:** - "Increase examples of collaboration with Sales" - "Automate all daily and weekly reporting" - "Increase customer visibility into new products, leading to expansion opportunities"	Unrealistic: "Increase NPS by 50 points this year." Not the *real* goal: "I want the new feature used by 50% of users." It's not the use of the feature that the customer desires, it's the *impact* on their business. Measure *that* instead. Not measurable: Ensure that whatever the customer states, it must be measurable, otherwise it should be considered a subjective goal. In the Weeds: "Sunset MySQL ETL" or similar jargon means nothing to the execs who ultimately sign the renewal. State what truly matters to them and the business impact. Nice-to-Haves: Challenge the customer if it is a must-have or nice-to-have. Ask about their strategic company and department priorities. Ask how they will be measured this quarter, this year. Ambiguous: "Better sales conversations" is wonderful, but how will you know if you've achieved it? Get specific.

then allow the group to adapt from there. For each business objective, challenge the customer to prioritize each one in relation to the others listed. Denote which stakeholder will benefit the most. Are there any obvious quick wins that surface? The best Success Plans for attaining the goal include key contributors and others responsible, both from your company and the customer.

Document the Plan

Record the detailed findings for each Objective separately in the Success Plan. Denote it as **Goal Value,** such as "Increase customer retention rate by 10% in the next fiscal year." Next, record the **Current Value** so you can measure progress each time you revisit the Success Plan. After that, categorize each goal as either **quantitative** or **qualitative.** If qualitative, make sure also to capture the subjective criteria by which success for that goal will be measured.

Track Value

You will want to track value and progression towards your customer's goal by following these three steps:

1. **Drive Progress.** Review the Success Plan at each handoff or Moment of Truth. Denote any change of ownership and validate each objective, including priority and attainability. Be sure to highlight the next steps and also review internally with your leadership. Leverage EBRs and other recurring meetings to keep up the momentum.
2. **Record and Demonstrate Success.** During EBRs and regular meetings, be sure to record any updates to each Objective and illustrate positive or trailing trends towards their goals. If a goal is attained, get confirmation from a customer that it has been achieved. The confirmation should be in writing or the form of an email. Then celebrate the accomplishment with the customer and share the good news internally.
3. **Validate and Update Business Objectives.** Businesses are dynamic environments. That means your customer's Success Plans will need to change mid-stream occasionally. Leverage automation and technology where possible by sending an email that lists objectives and related success criteria, asking them to validate it or comment accordingly. You can do this as an efficient iteration exercise before your next important meeting with your customer. Be sure also to keep track of when the specific objective was "last validated."

Finally, it is often said that Customer Success is a team sport. Equally, Success Plans require more than just you as the Customer Success Manager.

Figure 11.6   Success Plans: a cross-functional, collaborative process.

They require cross-functional collaboration within your company and most often involve your Services and Sales teams. **Figure 11.6** delineates how each respective team adds value to the creation of a successful plan. There could be other teams that have meaningful roles to play in Success Plans. For example, Product teams can enhance the product to achieve the goals sooner; Support can be involved with making sure launches go smoothly concerning any last-minute support cases.

Product Experience – Improving Your Product is Your #1 Priority

We've learned that getting your customers to their desired goals is something that should be done methodically by following the best practices of adoption management and Success Plans covered earlier in this chapter. Similarly, embracing a mindset of always helping your own company improve your product must be taken seriously by you. It's because Customer Success Managers tend to spend all day, every day, with customers. You are assisting customers, training customers, coaching and advising customers, and helping customers get value out of *the product.*

While the entirety of this book is devoted to the most important motions and activities of Customer Success Managers, the simple fact is they fundamentally help customers solve their business problems, using *the product.* It is precisely for this reason that Customer Success Managers must play a big part in helping products mature. As a Customer Success Manager, your *product* has to be the number one priority because your product is truly the single most critical reason customers are your customers.

All Success is Tied to the Product

No company can survive without having a good product. If you want to thrive, especially in SaaS, you need to have the best product in your market. Even further, trying to convince a customer that they can find value in a sub-par product, that doesn't fit their needs in the first place, goes against everything that Customer Success stands for. How can you make them successful with a product that does not work well for them?

We've heard our very own Customer Success trailblazer Dan Steinman say on many occasions, "If you are a really great Customer Success Manager, you might be able to squeeze out the first-year renewal solely based on the relationships you've built and the loyalties you've personally established. But you won't get a second renewal on the same grounds. **In the end, the only thing that will guarantee the renewal is whether or not the customer is getting value from *your product*.** This is why improving your product must be your number one priority." For a Customer Success Manager, this also means having an acute awareness of how the digital age is influencing customer expectations.

As a human consumer in the digital world, you know first-hand that technology has fueled consumer expectations at a remarkable pace. According to a *Wall Street Journal* article entitled "Customer experience is the key competitive differentiator in the digital age," "experiences that once delighted customers are soon routinely expected."[1] For example, getting WiFi during a flight used to be an innovative luxury. Now, people expect it and are dissatisfied if it's not available or if it's spotty.

As a Customer Success Manager, you have likely established regular meetings and business reviews with your primary customer contacts. Those select stakeholders should have a high-value experience as a result of your direct engagement with them. However, what about the hundreds or thousands of people working at your customer, that are using your product, and don't get the opportunity to interact with you? How do you, as a Customer Success Manager, deliver a great customer experience for all of them? Frankly, you simply can't. Ultimately, it is your product that provides the primary experience to all your customers. Your product is the primary vehicle for enabling customer outcomes at the individual level. Product is undoubtedly the most scalable way to deliver Customer Success.

CSMs and Product Teams Need Each Other

Now you might be telling yourself that improving the product experience is the job of the product team. While this may be true from an org-chart perspective, the reality is that Product teams need Customer Success teams and vice versa. Product groups are faced with the daunting task of knowing the needs of an entire market of customers while keeping an eye on future market opportunities for the business. They must do this while balancing the finite resources made available to them. For companies with hundreds of thousands of customers, it becomes increasingly difficult to have both the breadth and depth of intimately understanding the customer. Product teams are also expected to build products that help customers overcome change management barriers related to end-user product adoption.

The strength of Customer Success teams is their ability to tap into the depth of customer needs while also influencing change within customer organizations so that the value of the product can be realized. Creating a strong partnership with your Product team sets the foundation for creating product experiences that drive higher renewal rates and expansion opportunities.

Travis Kaufman understands the CS-to-Product relationship better than most. Travis is the Vice President of Growth at Gainsight. He shares: "It is important to realize that product and CS must work together to inform a more comprehensive product strategy. It's truly a team effort when comes to making the product the number one priority. In my career, I've learned that although your product strategy can be aligned with business objectives, it is not fully informed until you look closer into product usage patterns as a leading indicator of customer churn. You also need to have enough inputs from end-users."

Working with the Product Team

So, how can you create a trusted partnership between your CS and Product teams? First, you must establish two-way communication between teams. Product teams need to hear customer feedback and Customer Success teams need to understand how the product is evolving to meet customer needs. All too often, the two teams are only brought together during a time of crisis. *"Our biggest customer is churning because the product doesn't do XYZ. We have to do whatever it takes to save this customer!"* That too should sound familiar if you've spent any time in tech, even for a short while.

Active communication also encourages better adoption of new product capabilities. Establish a monthly (if you are a fast-growing start-up) or quarterly (if you are a larger organization with proven product-market fit) forum in which your Product team discusses new product features with the CS team. In that same forum, reserve time for the Customer Success team to proactively recommend new features that customers will value. This is also a great way to close the loop with specific customers when a feature they requested becomes available.

The second step is to define and monitor a success metric that both Product and Customer Success can share. The metric should be tied to performance evaluations and variable compensation, so each team is directly invested. The hint is not to select a lagging indicator, like customer churn. Rather, identify a leading indicator that captures the essence of whether customers are attaining value from the product, like Daily Active Users, which we introduced in the previous chapter.

The third tactic in establishing a trusted partnership between Customer Success and Product is to create a shared understanding of the future of your product direction. Product teams are in a state of constant discovery to validate the ideas worth pursuing from those that are not. Ultimately, you want this relationship to surface pervasive problems that customers have and are willing to pay for them to be solved. A tactical way Product teams accomplish this is the idea of beta programs – a pre-release of software that is given out to a group of users to try under real conditions. Customer Success teams can identify the right beta customers, and make sure that timely feedback from beta programs makes its way back to the Product teams.

If you have created a great and useful product to meet the needs of the customer, **and** you make the customer successful, that is not just embracing the idea of Customer Success: it is bringing it to its full potential.

●●●

Engaging customers is not a singular motion. It takes a symphony of players, each participating in unison, to help the customer attain their goals. We've learned that it requires relentless monitoring and managing of customers through their adoption phase, and intervening when their progress begins to stall. It also means having absolute clarity from your customer stakeholders on what success means and, more importantly, how it will be unilaterally measured.

Helping the customer, however, get to their goals won't be enough. You need to also focus on continuous improvement in your products and the experience your customers have of them. Product improvements are ultimately the most effective levers you can pull in terms of driving long-term value for your customers, at scale. How they learn to use your products is equally important, as is reducing the noise of content you provide to them. You need a system that creates the right content at just the right time for the right customer. Taking this holistic approach will help you in your quest of attaining your customer's success.

Endnote

1. Wladawsky-Berger, I. (2018). Customer experience is the key competitive differentiator in the digital age. *The Wall Street Journal* (20 April 2018). Retrieved from: https://blogs.wsj.com/cio/2018/04/20/customer-experience-is-the-key-competitive-differentiator-in-the-digital-age/.

12

Drive Revenue Growth Through Engagement, Proactive Risk Management, Churn Analysis, Expansion, and Advocacy

It is important to remember that customers are not a single entity but made up of multiple stakeholders who are decision-makers, functional owners, users, IT, and members of the C-suite. Each of these stakeholders can have a completely different definition of the outcome of value from your product. In this chapter, we'll share some best practices for managing these multi-stakeholder environments. We'll also cover some proven tactics for dealing with risks of your customers and, if possible, early enough to avoid cancelations and churns. If the customer does churn, it's equally important to learn from the experience to prevent future such scenarios. These are all critical processes for any Customer Success Manager.

Stakeholder Alignment: How to Manage Executive Sponsors and Other Customer Stakeholders

We often hear from Customer Success and Sales leaders that there are two common reasons for churn or downsell (revenue compression) of customers. **One:** an executive sponsor changes. **Two:** there is a lack of perceived value for your product or service among the Executive Sponsors. When you dig into these symptoms some more, the most actionable root causes turn out to be a few things:

- You, as a Customer Success Manager, were not aware of the shifting priorities at the customers' businesses.
- You did not keep up with the change in what "value" meant to them.
- Your company was not top of mind with executives.
- You were not engaged with multiple levels and key influencers within the customer organization.
- You were blindsided when your champions and sponsors left, especially in the high-volume and SMB segments where it's hard to keep tabs on all executive changes.

In response, we developed a Customer Success centric framework for operationalizing Executive Sponsorship programs. The purpose is clear: as your customers change priorities and shift strategies, maintaining alignment with customer executives and decision-makers becomes paramount to sustaining and driving growth for your organization while helping customers attain their goals. When executed well, it can also create opportunities for expansion (cross-sells and upsells). Simply follow the six recommended steps below to operationalize the process.

STEP 1: Define and Map Out the Key Personas

Similar to customer segmentation, you will want to identify people with related goals, needs, challenges, and motivations. With your customers,

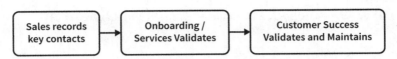

Figure 12.1   Identify and maintain key stakeholders.

that includes sponsors, buyers, system administrators, power users, and adoption champions. Your primary focus should be on decision-makers and influencers, as well as any potential "blockers." We also recommend adding a "persona" field to the Contacts table in your CRM. Here are some examples:

- CEO, CFO, COO – if they are critical to your buying decision.
- Sponsors, buyers – typically SVP or VP of functions that tend to use your product or service.
- Influencers – CIO, IT, Operations.
- System administrators and power users.
- Adoption champions – tend to be managers and directors of functional teams who can drive accelerated adoption of your offerings.

Now, follow the ideal flow illustrated in Figure 12.1 to operationalize the process.

STEP 2: Identify the Sponsor or "Buddy"

Identify the sponsor from your company that maps to these key personas. Determine which key personas should be matched to which buddies (e.g. Chief Customer Officers of mid-touch customers are matched to your VP of Customer Success). Similarly, you should map your CEO or COO to the sponsors at your largest enterprise customers. For your mid-market and SMB customers, you might have managers or directors from your team assigned as buddies to your customer's main influencers to get more scale. Configure your CRM to handle all of this metadata and automate where you can.

STEP 3: Operationalize a Regular Cadence of Outreaches

Leverage automation to create reminders and calls-to-action to remind your assigned buddies to reach out. Where you can, use a templated email that includes context about recent progress made or your company-wide updates. Even contemplate ghostwriting for your executives, so all they have to do is hit send, or send it on their behalf via an alias. Of course, encourage your buddies to add a more personal touch as appropriate. The goal is to get time for a quick call or meeting. However, be careful not to overdo it. You will have to throttle back and change criteria as your company and customer base grows. Finally, document notes from these outreaches for future reference and consider tracking successful stakeholder engagements as a Health Score measure. See Figures 12.2 and 12.3 for two examples of alignment and cadence.

STEP 4: Track your Buddy Outreaches

Executive-level contact, even if contentious, is a step in the right direction. Be sure to track all successful and unsuccessful stakeholder alignment engagements as a Health Score measure. Doing so, you will be able to see progress over time (see Figure 12.4).

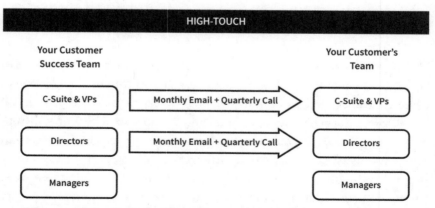

Figure 12.2   Stakeholder alignment and cadence for high-touch (Enterprise).

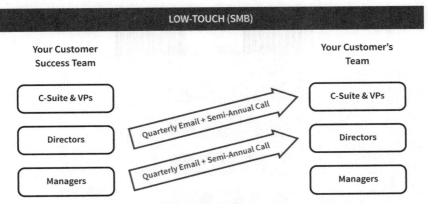

Figure 12.3   **Stakeholder alignment and cadence for low-touch (SMB).**

- Create an Engagement Score as part of your Health Score rubric that measures how often you connect with key personas at your customers.
- Track weekly improvements in the Engagement Score.
- Use one-on-ones to identify blockers for improving the score.

Risk Management: What to Do When a Customer is Trending Toward Cancelling: How to Proactively Escalate Risk and Save the Customer

Managing customer risk is something you will encounter every single day as a CSM. Learning how to react, maneuver, and escalate for help is critical to your success as well as your customers'. Hopefully, you work in a company culture that has empowered you to mitigate risks and raise the red flag without repercussions, all for the benefit of preventing customer churn. Even with the right culture, companies sometimes lack a process to identify customers at risk or, if it does exist, the data and related information are scattered between systems and across teams. The lack of operation can be a recipe that results in unexpected churn, the number one nemesis of CSMs. Additionally, CS teams can struggle with knowing what risks warrant escalation and instead find themselves in a perpetual firefighting mode, never actually able to focus on helping the customer attain their desired outcomes.

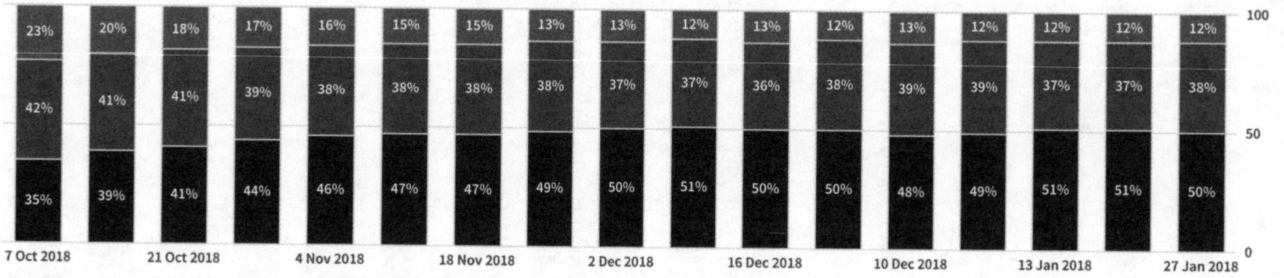

Figure 12.4   Stakeholder Engagements over time.

Let us turn, then, to steps for establishing a consistent and repeatable process to identify, monitor, escalate, and resolve risks, leveraging your leadership and cross-functional teams within your company.

STEP 1: Risk Framework

Define what constitutes a risk. Does the entire company know the definition? What are the categories and typical scenarios? What triggers them? Do you have data and a system in place that can be used to notify you when predetermined thresholds have been met automatically? Do you have a centralized place to track manually created risks? As rudimentary as it may seem, make sure your organization understands the difference between risk and escalation. As shown in Figure 12.5, a *risk* is something not going as planned. These frequently happen because situations change at your company and each of your customers. CSMs will be able to address most of these risks. However, every so often there will be risks that need attention and help from other functions in your company. These are called *escalations*.

It is also important to denote the common myths of risks and escalations. They are:

- NOT an indicator of job performance. Take comfort here. There is always a subset of your managed customers that are at risk. It is part of

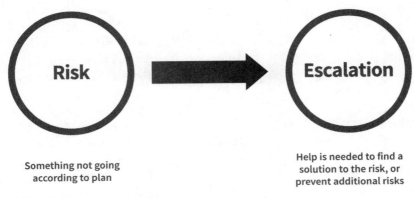

Something not going
according to plan

Help is needed to find a
solution to the risk, or
prevent additional risks

Figure 12.5   Risk versus escalation.

the job as a Customer Success Manager, and you should not internalize it as a sign of poor personal performance. In fact, some CSMs are so good at managing risk and turning customers around that they are specifically assigned these accounts.

- NOT a secret. Do not try to conquer the world on your own. Great team members identify risks early and communicate often!
- NOT to be considered additional work. You have an entire company of people who also don't want to see any customer churn. You will be surprised how much they are willing to help, even if it's a five-minute consult with your resident expert. In turn, you'll do the same when you're asked to help with other customer escalations. Your company, not CSMs, wins, keeps, and loses customers. You are in this together.
- NOT optional. You are not doing your job if you are not proactively identifying and escalating risks.

When designing your Risk Framework, establish common categories. See Table 12.1 for examples:

Table 12.1 Risk categories matrix.

Risk Category	Owner	Trigger	Examples
Deployment	CSM	Auto	License utilization 25% below benchmark
Engagement	CSM	Auto	No executive engagement in 3 months
Adoption	CSM	Auto	25% reduction in active users vs. 3 months ago
ROI/Value	CSM	Auto	Customer not seeing any ROI
Overall	CSM	Auto	Detractor/Passive NPS
Support	Support	Auto	Number of open support risks significantly higher than x-day rolling average
Sentiment	CSM	Auto or Manual	Customer stakeholders unhappy, disengaged, unresponsive
External	CSM	Manual	Loss of customer stakeholders; Merger and Acquisition activities, Financial risks

STEP 2: First Responses and Escalation Paths

For each risk and scenario defined in Step 1, what is the first play you will run? What's your first response? Who owns it? How and when should they escalate it? Which are the right people and teams to engage for help and notification? You will need to create standard playbooks and escalation paths accordingly. The steps you define will, of course, be different for each scenario and unique to each company. However, there are some universal escalation paths to consider and some simple rules to follow:

- Escalation paths define how and when risks should be escalated, and to whom, to ensure the right people are engaged.
- In an escalation, you are requesting action, not merely informing the recipient.
- Understand which type of escalation path is right for your company and the situation (see Figure 12.6). In most cases, we recommend a hybrid approach that is linear but allows for exceptions, especially in highly sensitive circumstances or when decisions need to be made quickly.

Defining when to escalate is another critical step. Here are some common examples that warrant escalation:

- The customer expresses **FRUSTRATION**: "Why is this taking so long?" and "This is urgent." It could be a negative tone in an email or during a phone call.
- The customer requests **ESCALATION** for an issue they are having.

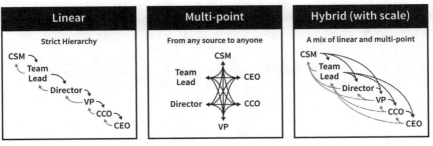

Figure 12.6   Three types of escalation paths.

- The customer is **NON-RESPONSIVE** for **five** business days unless there's a known reason (e.g. vacation, end of quarter).
- **RENEWAL** is in process, and the date is imminent.
- **INTERNAL ESCALATION** from your peer teammates, like Support, Services, or Sales.
- No clear path forward or **ETA TO RESOLUTION.**
- If you are ever in doubt or do not feel fully equipped to manage the risk on your own, **ESCALATE!**

STEP 3: Ongoing Process and People Involvement

Create clear and easily understood processes and rubrics for everyone to follow. Include a variety of examples and publish an FAQ. Do not leave it unattended for too long; revisit your risk management process regularly, so it aligns with the evolution of your team and company. To effectively manage a risk escalation process will require active involvement and commitment across your organization, including heavy CSM participation with dedicated time to discuss escalated risks during weekly one-on-one or team meetings (see Figure 12.7).

Reduce Churn with a Deep Understanding of Why Your Customers Have Left

One of the best ways to understand your customer churn is not to think about it in terms of retention or the lack thereof. Rather, view churn as

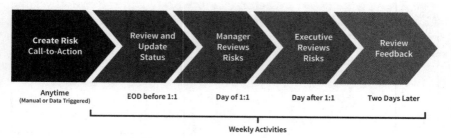

Figure 12.7   Risk escalation process.

a teaching moment and as an opportunity to learn deeply about how to prevent it. Ask yourself, "How can I use this otherwise negative event, to rise to a higher level of proactive engagement with my remaining and future customers?"

When a customer decides to no longer be your customer, it is your and your company's responsibility to find out why. Many steps led to the customer's churn, and there is a significant amount of valuable data to be gathered. However, you can't just go in expecting customers to open up about their experience. Customers often feel a wide range of emotions when churn happens: aggravation, betrayal, relief, embarrassment, failure, frustration, and anger, to name a few. The challenge is that most people are not well-trained in navigating these often uncomfortable conversations with customers while also drawing out the root-causes of churn.

Every single customer who churns should be interviewed. While someone from your company will likely want to reach out directly to the customer to draw out the why, it's actually a best practice to use an outside agency or an anonymous well-written survey to solicit unbiased feedback about what really happened. That's because there's an art to getting the customer to reveal the real reasons they churned.

If you've exhausted every option to try to keep them as your customer, you will need to pivot quickly to understand their reasons for leaving. If you don't have the luxury of using a third-party firm, you must learn to tread lightly, approach the customer with compassion and never be defensive. Remember, every churned customer has the potential to come back in the future as a new customer. So, how you handle this exit is vital to your company's reputation and future opportunities.

Rarely is there a "blind churn": a customer who left you when you weren't expecting it at all. You'll need to work diligently to discover the root cause. Was there a launch risk where the customer didn't make it through onboarding in a timely fashion? Did their executive sponsor leave the company and you didn't know about it? Did the users not adopt your solution nor make it part of their regular workflow? Did the product not meet their needs? Did they choose a competitor or go back to a manual process?

Even if the customer reveals their specific reasons for departing, there should always be an internal examination of other contributing factors to help you conclude the root causes of the churn. Some refer to this exercise as a post-mortem. But it's more like reverse-engineering the churn through the lens of the customer and their journey with your company. You are carefully deconstructing the customer's experience with your product and your processes to examine and analyze it in detail to discover systemic factors and failures. The goal? To ensure that the same situation never happens again with any current or future customer.

We were fortunate at Gainsight to have partnered with a firm that specializes in customer discovery and churn interviews, which we used for our customers. Yes, even awesome companies with amazing products have occasional churn. The interview results were compiled in a sizable report and sent directly to our CEO. He soon began to distribute it to every person in the company, with a mandatory directive to read it and to do so without a spirit of accusation or blame. WOW! Talk about a transparent and open opportunity to learn from failure. These reports were incredibly insightful. Sometimes they were unpleasant to read, especially if it was an account you owned or were heavily involved with. They portrayed moments that were emotional for the customer, especially that of frustration or disappointment because those very customers wanted to succeed using your product. It's why they selected you over your competitors.

What was always fascinating about these reports was that the interviewer was able to draw out an amazing level of detail and unfiltered commentary from customers. With that in mind, we were absolutely compelled to bring you the very person responsible for elevating our appreciation for the art of interviewing for the purpose of churn analysis: Alan Armstrong, CEO at Eigenworks. Alan built a team dedicated to drawing out the real stories from companies.

We are truly blessed to have him provide you with useful and actionable tips to consider for your customers, as you turn your churnings into learnings.

Tragically, this would be one of Alan's last opportunities to share his amazing and gifted insights with the world. Alan passed away suddenly, days before our manuscript was due to our publisher. He was literally the first person we asked to be a guest contributor. He was elated at the opportunity and worked so diligently to give you the best he could. It is our honor to immortalize his words here among our own.

Your Customers Are Lying to You: Getting the Real Story on Why Your Customers Churn

By Alan Armstrong, CEO at Eigenworks

Your Shared Beliefs Get in the Way

Although root causes of churn may not sound earth-shattering, they can be difficult to diagnose precisely because of internal biases about what people *presume* is the problem. Root causes often have company-wide implications. Team dynamics and intense pressures to perform can make it more difficult to gain the alignment necessary to address the underlying causes. But there is a way to break through the internal noise and pivot externally. Ultimately, you have to establish an open and unfiltered dialog with the customer and speak with a large enough sample of customers to identify patterns that apply broadly. You will have to reach beyond survey and usage data and be ready to set aside personal preconceptions of why your customers are churning.

Uncover the story using Structured Dialog: Buyer as Hero™

Getting the story behind churn requires you to get inside the customer's world, and to do that, you need dialog, over the phone or in person. While that sounds simple, it can be challenging. Even when you do get them on the phone, it's hard not to bring your bias to the table. Finally, as much as you work to remove your bias, your colleagues in other departments may discount your insights because of your *perceived* bias.

With these challenges in mind, we have developed and refined an effective dialog model that helps to remove bias and disarm the defensive customer, shared here for you to consider applying to your own customers.

The model, which we call *Buyer-as-Hero™*, puts your buyer in the lead role of the story. The buyer is the primary person that has championed driving change at your customer's organization. It takes you and your product out of the center of the story. It focuses on your customer instead. It enables you to ask questions like, "What motivated the

(continued)

(*continued*)

change when they originally chose your product?", "What outcomes were they trying to achieve?", "How did they get from there to here?", and "What can be learned from that journey?"

Step 1: Change the Conversation, Get into Research Mode

It can be incredibly difficult for CSMs to convince customers to participate in exit interviews. By the time they cancel, most of your churned customers have moved on, and many feel that they've tried to give you their feedback already.

Frankly, you need to reset the conversation with the customer. However, it should be handled by someone other than the CSM. It can be helpful to create a dedicated function for customer research, but this doesn't have to be over complicated or even full-time. It could be an individual or even a group in or outside of CS that can dedicate some time to the task. When you approach the customer, be explicit that you are conducting research, and not trying to re-engage them. Do NOT treat these calls like a sales campaign.

The other reset is in your own mindset. Do whatever you can to remove your own bias. Your goal is to have the customer tell you *their story* and diagnose it from there.

Step 2: Get the Self-Reported Story

Nancy's company had been the leader in their industry. Their revenue and stock price grew at impressive rates. But when Nancy called me, she was worried. She had been asked to examine why customers were switching to a competitor, an alternative that, until recently, nobody had considered being a threat. Her initial scan identified about $15M in churned revenue, which included some big-named logos.

We begin all interviews with what we call the self-reported story in which customers tell their own version of what happened, and why, without guidance from the interviewer. We want the unfiltered version. In this phase, you are a journalist, digging for the truth.

The self-reported story for Nancy's customers was pretty brutal. We heard stories about bad service, products that were discontinued without a transition plan, and aggressive sales tactics that alienated customers. It wasn't hard to get these stories. We just had to *open the faucet*, ask for their story in the right way, and listen well.

It's not always that easy. Nancy's team had tried, and tried, to get these stories themselves. But by the time their customers had switched to their competitor, they had no interest and would not make the time for Nancy's team to learn. This is not surprising because there is an inherent obstacle when trying to learn on your own about churn from your customers. You are perceived as trying to revive the account. Whether or not it's true, that is the perception. Even if customers agree to talk, they are likely to provide convenient answers like, "Oh, our budget went away," rather than giving you the whole story because they are simply avoiding being pitched to again.

To overcome this strong bias held by your churned customer, you need to put the customer into the role of hero and engage the customer in storytelling. That requires us to stop using words like "Why?" Think about a recent unexpected churned customer. The first and most prolific question everyone in your company was asking is, "Why?" The problem is that word puts the buyer in the mode of justifying their decision. Instead, you simply want them to tell their story. Can you do it without asking or using the word "WHY?"

Step 3: Build Trust

When the customer begins to share their story, nudge them further. When they complain, we say "yes" or "I understand" to affirm what they are telling you. I often say that our job here is to talk the customer *into* their opinions, with lines such as, "Yes, I hear you. That makes sense. Tell me more . . ."

It is critical at this stage to continue as an investigative journalist, listening without adding to the story. Keep digging. "Is there more?" "Why was that important?" And so on. Get even more specific, "I see your Health Score was green during this specific timeframe. What did we miss?"

(continued)

(*continued*)

When you believe you have the whole story, mirror it back. Try to synthesize what you heard from the customer without simply repeating their words, starting with a phrase like, "It seems like . . . ."

If you've done well listening and encouraging your customer's storytelling, they may lean in further and begin revealing more relevant details. When you hear phrases like, "To be totally honest with you," that's when you know you're getting the real scoop!

Step 4: Test Your Practices and Beliefs with "What About . . .?" Questions

Most Customer Success teams do everything they can to intervene well before the renewal event or, at worse, the churn notice happens. It can be hard, then, to listen patiently while the customer talks about their disappointing experience.

However, if you have your churned customer still engaged, that means you've established enough trust in the call to explore more directed questions. Make a list of all of the things that *should have* helped the customer succeed, and get ready to ask them. We call these "What about" questions, because many of them can start with those two words.

"What about our onboarding process?" "What about your QBR?" Or, from the product perspective, "What about feature X; was that explained to you?"

The "What About" questions provide hints of things that you could have possibly fixed or addressed. While you can't be 100% certain the customer still would have stayed, you now have insights to apply to your current customers to ensure they don't have similar experiences.

Step 5: Test Decision Strength: "What If . . .?"

With the story now clearly in mind, you can begin to test hypothetical interventions. "What if the product had done X?" Or "What if we had been able to get in touch when we noticed that you were offline for a week?" You can now explore whether those interventions would have helped to retain the customer. Be careful here because hypothetical questions are tricky for a few reasons. First, they can be unreliable because buyers don't actually know what they would have done with a change in circumstances. Because of that potential, discern carefully anything that the customer claims would have caused them to stay with you. If you hear "Had you called me when I was in trouble, I would have stayed with you." If you start hearing that same message from other customers, then you know it's not simply a biased perspective.

Step 6: Get More Stories! How Many Stories Before We Can Trust a Pattern?

It is tempting, but irresponsible, to react to a single customer story. Certainly, if a customer is in trouble and can be assisted, escalate that situation. But you need to have several conversations with several customers before you can have confidence that you understand what's really going on systemically.

How many conversations? From our experience, 20 conversations is a magic number. If you talk to eight people, you are probably getting five or six distinct ideas, and it's hard to tell whether the two or three that match each other are a pattern or just a coincidence.

The goal is to reach something that qualitative researchers call *saturation*. Saturation means that the next story is likely to sound like one of the previous stories. When does that happen? There are many opinions on this, ranging from 6 to 50 interviews, but in our assessment, it is about 20 conversations that are needed.

A Word about Customer Segments

Just because you have 20 conversations doesn't mean they are applicable across your entire market. You likely have several customer segments. If that's the case, you need to treat each segment separately. You may not need a full 20 conversations in each segment, but, for example, trying to treat financial services and healthcare with the same study is likely to be misleading.

(continued)

(continued)

Should You Do This Yourself, or Hire?

Whenever clients ask me how much win/loss or churn research they should do on their own, I answer, "as much as possible." I think it's incredibly important to have and retain a good churn-research model in-house.

However, there are serious limitations to the DIY (do-it-yourself) approach. Even if your team has the time and experience conducting and analyzing a sufficient number of customer conversations, *it can be hard to shed your bias as the builder, seller, and supporter of your product.* Consider that for a moment. It's hard for vendors to convince churned customers to open up, or even take a call. Customers feel they've sent you enough signals already, and you pursuing them after they've cancelled is perceived as poor taste and considered too little, too late.

The other bias you face is an internal one. No matter who takes on the job of research, other teams tend to discount the findings because the researcher is seen to have an agenda. An outside firm can help to eliminate that bias.

Step 7: Success Interviews, Not Just Churn

You need to study your successful customers and customer engagements just as diligently as you try to find the root causes of churn. Don't assume that you know why they are successful. In particular, focus on three things: the vision for change, customer profile, and what helped them overcome the aspects of your product that cause others to struggle.

With success interviews, you can find out what your best customers are doing with your product and why they value it. What do those customers have in common? Can you find more like them? Knowing the answers to these questions will help you do a better job of understanding churn. You'll even learn that some of your churned customers should have been disqualified before they purchased because they simply were not a good fit and, even if they wanted, could not have achieved their goals with your product.

> Even well-qualified, geared-up customers need to overcome challenges to succeed with your product. What made them successful, and how do they compare to churned customers?

Alan's valuable message is often overlooked. Interviewing your former customers is an incredible way to turn a negative into a positive – or going from churning to learning. We are thankful for Alan's lesson that our losses can be an education. It begins with a conversation with a human being, building trust, and listening to the customer's story. The gift of listening, once again, comes to the fore as one of the greatest skills you can have as a CSM. It must be embraced, encouraged, and used properly to benefit you, your company, and most of all, the customer.

Expansion Management: Understanding White Space in Your Customer Base to Upsell and Cross-sell Your Products and Services

When a developed, mature customer finds value in your product, they will have greater value and trust in your relationship. The customer will be open to gain more from their partnership with you. It is a natural and logical progression for them to want to buy more products, new features, additional licenses, and thus create more recurring revenue. The responsibility of Customer Success is to keep customers in a position to accomplish those things.

Let's consider our counterpart on the Sales team. Every single activity a Sales Rep performs increases the potential of closing a deal and, thus, drive sales. Now, compare that with Customer Success. It's an organization that most often is positioned on the org-chart separately from Sales. However, the goal of Customer Success is, and always will be, to empower and enable more sales to happen. While not as overt as Sales, those deals come in the form of renewals, upsells, and cross-sells from happy, engaged, and loyal customers that you, the CSM have curated.

As we reported earlier, Customer Success Managers are taking on direct commercial responsibilities. As such, it is important for you to have a baseline understanding of the concepts and motions related to expansion. There are two types of expansions: *upsells* and *cross-sells*.

- An "upsell" is commonly understood to be selling more of the same offering to an existing customer or business unit.
- A "cross-sell" typically requires a new sales cycle because, while it may be the same offering, it is to a new business unit in an existing organization or it may be an entirely new offering to an existing customer or business unit.
- "White space" represents all of the opportunities for expansion.

The strategy is to implement a process to identify and act on an upsell and cross-sell potential. This inevitably requires the use of technology, data, and collaboration with your sales organization to ensure ownership and rules of engagement are in place. More than ever, CSMs are being held to an expansion metric which often includes surfacing and acting on expansion opportunities. If they aren't receiving direct commissions, they will most certainly expect some level of attribution, credit, or recognition for the discovery.

Below are a few of the most important things you must understand as a CSM when identifying expansion opportunities (see Table 12.2).

- How does your company make money from your customers?
- What types of "widgets" do they purchase?

Table 12.2   Example types of expansion.

	Upsell	Cross-sell
All businesses	Licenses, devices, or locations	Features Additional or Premium services
Software as a service	Hours of services or training entitled capacity	Additional products
On-premise businesses	Product version/upgrades services upgrades	Additional products
Consumption businesses	Entitled consumption/ capacity	

- Do you know all the offerings of your company well enough to at least identify potential opportunities you could pass to a seasoned Sales Rep?
- What data from a customer could give you an indication that one of these opportunities exist?
- Have they deployed or used most of their "widgets"?

Reportability is equally important to any process you establish. Create a dashboard for managing the expansion pipeline. You read that correctly. As a CSM, you very well may be managing your expansion-sales pipeline (while still being partnered with a Sales Rep). Below are some of the essential data points that should be included, which means you'll need to ensure you are capturing them somewhere reportable.

A table showing open expansion opportunities:
- Customer Name
- Expansion Value
- Expected Close Date (sorted, soonest at the top)
- Notes from the most recent Timeline entry
- Link to the most recent Timeline entry.

A stacked bar chart showing open expansion CTAs:
- Values: Expansion Value
- Bars: Calendar Month of Expected Close Date
- Stacked Series: Forecast Category.

A table showing forecast categories that changed in the previous week:
- Customer Name
- Expansion Value
- Expected Close Date (sorted, soonest at the top)
- Forecast Category Before
- Forecast Category After.

You will also want to follow best practices for forecasting each opportunity. If your organization has not defined probabilities yet, the model shown in Table 12.3 may be a good starting point:

Table 12.3   Probability forecasting.

Criteria	Default probability of win
Emailed decision–maker	0%
Discussion with decision–maker	20%
Contract sent	50%
Verbal commit	80%
Signed contract (closed won)	100%
Lost (closed lost)	0%

The White Space or Expansion Opportunity dashboard should be integrated into the regular flow of work and internal meetings with your leadership. Table 12.4 calls out the three most important CSM expansion management dashboards specifically intended to help track and drive additional revenues from within the portfolio of customers you manage.

Advocacy Management: How to Turn Your Best Customers into Evangelists

We know that happy customers, when achieving their desired outcomes, are the only ones genuinely willing to refer your company, product, or service to friends, family, or colleagues. Customer advocacy starts on the first day of the Customer Lifecycle with the intent of creating a Customer Advocate. Moreover, the advantages of an advocacy program can be felt across the enterprise and especially in Sales and Marketing. The benefits of an advocacy program are evidenced in research from the *Harvard Business Review* which showed that 84% of B2B buyers are now starting the purchasing process with a referral, and peer recommendations are influencing more than 90% of all B2B buying decisions.[1]

As such, Customer Success Managers are uniquely positioned to turn your customers into advocates of your company. As an organization, you should implement all of the following ingredients of a successful advocacy

Table 12.4 CSM Expansion Management dashboards.

Dashboard	Purpose	Summary
Exec Manager Dashboard for weekly meetings	How are we tracking with our upsell and cross-sell opportunities? Are there any opportunities where the exec/mgr can step in?	▪ Upsell/cross-sell opportunities by stage
CSM Dashboard for weekly 1:1s	What accounts have expansion potential? How much potential revenue is tied up in these accounts? Based on these two factors, which accounts should I prioritize?	▪ White Space Report ▪ $$ of pipeline created in upsell category by Oppty stage ▪ # opportunities in cross-sell by Oppty stage ▪ $$ of pipeline created in upsell category by Oppty stage ▪ # of opportunities in upsell by Oppty stage ▪ # of CTAs (CSM)
ROI Dashboard	What is the impact, on revenue and GRR, of identified expansion opportunities?	▪ Closed revenue from opportunities created via cross-sell and upsell

program, but you can certainly start with any number of them and build out from there.

1. **Deliver value: Just do it!**
2. **Demonstrate Value: Show you did it!**

Table 12.5   Examples of customer success qualified advocacy.

CSQL	CSQA-only
▪ Renewal	▪ Case studies
▪ Upsells	▪ Improved adoption
▪ Cross-sells	▪ Increased Health Score
▪ Referrals	▪ Completed training
	▪ Testimonials and third-party reviews
	▪ NPS promoter
	▪ Speaking at your events

3. **Establish advocacy milestones.** Okay, we'll explain this one. Because you will get "credit" for anything bad that happens to your customer, you better take credit for everything good. Every one of the events or milestones listed in Table 12.5 should be considered either a Customer Success Qualified Advocacy (CSQA) or a Customer Success Qualified Leads (CSQL) if they were sourced directly from you, the CSM. Similar to a Marketing Qualified Lead (MQL) or Sales Qualified Lead (SQL), a CSQL is a considerably higher value lead because it comes from an existing customer and generally appreciates a higher probability of a closed sale. At Gainsight, our Customer Success Team establishes quarterly targets for CSQAs and CSQLs because we know all of the listed activities are leading indicators of portfolio growth and overall good health.

4. **Identify likely advocates:** utilize your Health Scores and technology to quickly and easily identify customers based on usage, sentiment, and NPS, value achieved, engagement, willingness to advocate, Success Plan progress, and active engagement with your marketing and community events or online forums.

5. **Manage sales references:** find a way to easily report which are your best customers and which ones are eligible for providing references. Be sure not to overuse them and always seek their permission first.

6. **Promote and reward your advocates:** we asked Customer Success Advocacy thought-leader Chad Horenfeldt, VP of Client Success at Updater, to provide additional color on this topic:

Advocacy rewards your most loyal and supportive customers as it provides them with opportunities to attend and speak at events, to have their names highlighted in industry publications or on your website, and to gain access to influential people in your company and industry. Giving them some of your swag can also go a long way. Advocacy shows that you care and appreciate them. It's a secret weapon that can help retain and grow your most strategic customers. By creating this type of reciprocal relationship, you can confidently count on your advocates to help you when you need it — whether it's mentioning your company to their colleagues or providing a key reference to seal your next deal.

7. **Report the impact:** create and establish a dashboard that illustrates some level of revenue attribution to all your good work as a CSM. A dashboard can be easily accomplished by adding a couple of fields on the Sales Opportunity Record to include CSM Name and CSQA Type. Now there's an awesome report for your CS Leader to present to the Board of Directors.

●●●

We have covered the history and the essential skills and competencies required of the Customer Success Manager's job function. We have also outlined the various activities that will be encountered on a daily basis as a CSM. Now it's time to shift to the leaders of Success teams and provide some insights and best practices unique to managing a team of often very diverse CSMs.

Endnote

1. Minsky, L. and Quesenberry, K. (2016). How B2B sales can benefit from social selling. *Harvard Business Review* (8 November 2016).

PART IV

Retaining and Developing the Best CSMs

13

Managing a Customer Success Team

Up until this point, we have covered the core skills and processes that a Customer Success Manager needs to practice and internalize. It's time to shift focus toward the leaders of Customer Success teams. They have an equally important responsibility to make sure they hire, develop, lead, and retain the best talent in the organization. To do this, you need to be introduced to three main concepts. The first concept is how to manage the CSM workload and coverage ratios depending on your segmentation strategy. Then, how to design incentive structures to drive the right behaviors. The final concept is how to use reports and dashboards to drive operational rigor.

Segmentation and Aligning a Customer Success Manager to the Right Customer

Earlier in the book, we briefly covered segmentation, but we feel it is a subject that requires a bit more knowledge and depth to use it effectively. Your goal is to provide a balanced CSM-to-customer ratio (or CSM ratio) based on your business segmentation strategy. Your company likely has a wide range of customers with varying sizes, revenue, expansion opportunities, and needs. To be able to manage such a diverse group of customers, it is essential to segment them into subgroups based on shared characteristics. In Chapter 7 (Figure 7.4), we reported that the most common data point for segmenting customers is an Annual Recurring Revenue (ARR) number. If your business doesn't have a recurring revenue business model, an alternative is to use "expected revenue" from your customer. A revenue-related metric is the most commonly used because customer-based revenue tends to be an exceptional proxy for the CSM workload, especially as it relates to meetings, touchpoints, and escalations.

Segmentation assignments for your CSMs are an important strategy for a company of any size, especially as the company starts to grow. The worst thing you can do is have a segmentation model that both inhibits your CSM's capabilities and your growth. We decided to approach two people for their rich understanding of this subject. The first is Patrick Eichen, Vice President of Client Success at Cornerstone OnDemand. Patrick has vast experience developing operationally efficient, development-driven, and performance management models in Customer Success.

According to Patrick, "Customer segmentation is one of the most important aspects of scaling customer success. Investing time and resources in this area will help you better understand your customers and how your product provides them value. Most importantly, it should help to clearly define what they need from you in order to be successful. As you start to refine this approach, you will likely realize that the skills needed for a Customer Success Manager to be successful in supporting each customer segment will look different. Aligning the right type of CSM to the right customer becomes a critical component of the overall framework."

Patrick added that Cornerstone spent much time identifying customer personas in each of their market segments, which influences their segmentation approach. Aside from just focusing on typical aspects like revenue, employee population, and industry, Cornerstone also considered factors such as how mature customer talent processes were and how complex the customer use-case was with Cornerstone's software. "Having implemented thousands of customers," Patrick said, "Cornerstone now has a good sense of what type of support our clients will typically need and have incorporated this in how we have scaled customer success."

The second individual we sought out to enlighten us on this subject was David Kocher. David is the Vice President of Customer Success at GE Digital. GE Digital is the leading software company for the industrial Internet. They have been reimagining the industry's infrastructure by connecting software, apps, and analytics to industrial businesses. David and his team have gone beyond using the revenue and ARR model and contemplated using a "needs" based segmentation. They set out to answer a few questions that dictated their segmentation strategy:

A. Which customers should I engage with?
B. When should I engage with them?
C. What do I focus on during my engagement with them?

David told us that "While difficult, answering these questions is critical if your program is going to be successful." The subsequent sections highlight the approach utilized at GE Digital for addressing this need. They call this simple segmentation **"Prioritize to Execute"** (Figure 13.1).

David explained that the first half of this approach, the Prioritize section, addresses question A, "which customers" and question B, "when to engage." To segment for prioritization, they used two axes: Value and Health. These two dimensions are central to prioritization because they tell you who's valuable and how happy they are. Grouping customers into these buckets is straightforward, but the insights gleaned are meaningful. You can structure the CS organization or your portfolio of accounts for the highest impact. According to David, to structure a CS organization using this technique, it's essential to identify what the appropriate coverage ratios are to enable optimal engagement with each grouping: Immediate, Fast, On Schedule.

- **Immediate** – requires a rapid response from a CSM with targeted skills (product, industry) at a lower ratio given the size, and presumable complexity, of customers with higher ARR.
- **Fast** – requires a quick response from a CSM with general skills at a higher ratio given the reduced complexity of lower ARR customers.
- **On Schedule** – requires a gated response from a CSM to align needed activities with the Customer's Journey and defined complexity. Coverage ratios for this group vary based on the Customer Lifecycle stage and size.

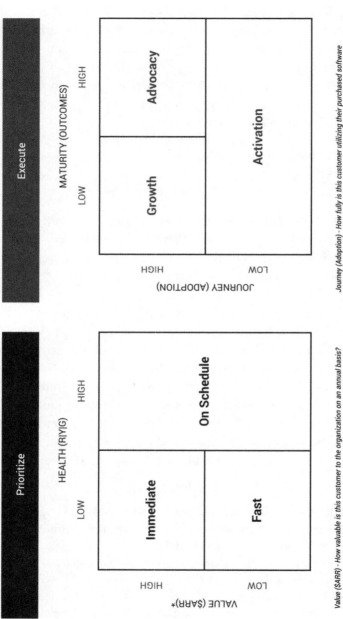

Value ($ARR) - How valuable is this customer to the organization on an annual basis? (*should also augment with qualitative inputs)

Health (R|Y|G) - How much risk (of churn, of bad publicity ...) is present based on issues or concerns this customer is experiencing?

Journey (Adoption) - How fully is this customer utilizing their purchased software (licenses/subscription and functionality)?

Maturity (Outcomes) - How much benefit is this customer realizing from their utilization of the software?

Figure 13.1 GE Digital's framework for segmentation.

"By determining how many customers you have in each bucket," David stated, "you can calculate how many Customer Success Managers, with what skills, will be required to save customer's with low health while progressing higher health customers along the adoption maturity curve. This simple segmentation won't work for 100% of your accounts. There will be additional qualitative criteria you need to review for exceptional customers to determine the coverage model."

As a CSM managing a portfolio of customers, you will find that accounts move within the segmentation – hopefully from left to right. Low health, therefore, is a prioritization gating mechanism. Putting out customer fires, quickly, so you can move toward higher-value interactions is a must. This move requires a balancing act of managing the critical few that are escalated while still accelerating adoption for customers with positive health indicators.

The second half of this approach answers question C: "what to do." As noted above, if the customer has low health, the most critical play is focused on risk remediation. Remediation plays should consider the nature of the issue (product, support, delivery, and commercial) to develop a specific plan of attack. The plan must be agreed to by the account team and the customer. Remediation plans should be tracked regularly to completion.

For those customers not at risk, GE deploys the "Execute" segmentation to determine specific playbooks or "plays" to run. They leverage two axes – Journey and Maturity – to group customers based on how much they are using your software and how much value they're receiving by doing so.

- Activation plays – supporting the Customer Journey with onboarding, adoption enablement, performance tracking, and other similar activities.
- Growth plays – retaining and growing account value through upsells and cross-sells.
- Advocacy plays – evangelizing the benefit of engagement, both internally and externally.

Finally, Patrick suggests that if and when you consider a Customer Success segmentation strategy for your organization, start by asking yourself the following questions:

- What is our go-to-market strategy, and where do we expect our customer base to grow?
- What are the shared characteristics of our customers? Size, industry, use-case with our product?
- What are the most common support needs for each customer segment? Are we addressing them in the right way today?
- How do we measure success? Do the measures align with our customer's vision of success?
- What are the skills needed for a CSM to be successful in each customer segment?

Determining the Best Customer Success Manager-to-Customer Ratio and CSM Profiles

We now know that most companies think about their customer base in three segments and use revenue as the basis for segmenting their customers, typically into High-, Medium-, and Low-revenue customers. The next thing we need to understand is how company resources, namely CSMs, are allocated. Are they driving maximum success across these segments and in the most cost-effective manner possible? How many customers does a CSM effectively manage?

Enterprise Customer Success Manager-to-Customer Ratio and CSM Profiles

Based on our prior research, some patterns emerged with regards to how companies segment their customers. In the Enterprise segment, which has your highest revenue customers, the median amount of Annual Recurring Revenue (ARR) that an Enterprise CSM manages is $2M to $5M. Meaning that CSMs assigned to this segment manage a customer portfolio size between $2M–$5M of ARR with a median number of customers between 11–50 (Figure 13.2).

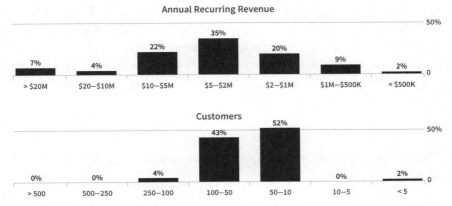

Figure 13.2 Enterprise Customer Success Manager – ARR managed and customer ratios.

In the Enterprise segment, you typically want CSMs who are experienced at managing the complexities of these types of customers. The skills usually include managing a wide range of stakeholders in the same organization, such as different Business Units' stakeholders, and various functional stakeholders. They will also need executive-presence and must drive significant change management with customers. In some circumstances, you might find value in bringing in experts with specific industry verticals or categories that a majority of your Enterprise customers belong to, as we described in Chapter 4. Profiles of persons with prior experience with these skills include Management Consultants, Enterprise Sales, Account Management, Enterprise Project Managers, and Enterprise Solutions Consultants or Engineers.

At Cornerstone, Patrick has been very thoughtful about the types of people they hire as Enterprise Customer Success Managers. He stated that: "In our large enterprise customer segment, our clients invest a considerable amount to implement our software. They have a greater degree of complexity, and in most cases, our product is a critical component of their entire talent management process. They expect daily support from someone with a high degree of expertise, and we incorporate this into how we ensure they have the right CSM to work with. We partner them with someone who has a significant track record of experience and has the right mixture of technical savvy, deep industry expertise, and account management skill set to guide them to the right outcome. These are often individuals that have held senior positions in industry and in some cases have implemented our product before. We do everything we can to create an environment where our customers feel like their CSM has walked in their shoes and is a true extension of their team."

Mid-Market Customer Success Manager-to-Customer Ratio and CSM Profiles

In the Mid-Market segment, the industry trend shows a CSM managing roughly the same amount of ARR as an Enterprise Customer Success Manager, but it is spread across many more customers.

The median amount of Annual Recurring Revenue (ARR) that a Mid-Market Customer Success Manager manages is also between $2M to $5M, with 58% of Mid-Market Customer Success Managers managing more than $2M of ARR (Figure 13.3). A Mid-Market Customer Success Manager manages roughly 100–250 customers as the median. As you can imagine, it becomes hard for this segment to offer the same human workflows as the Enterprise segment. Hence, it's essential to be more

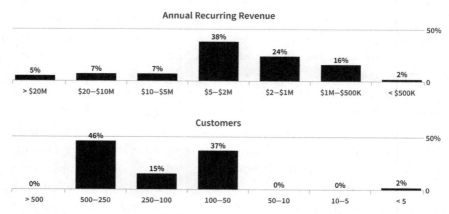

Figure 13.3   Mid-Market Customer Success Manager – ARR managed and customer Ratios.

"digital first" in the outreach strategy and rely on human intervention on a "just in time" basis.

In the Mid–Market segment, you typically want CSMs who are skilled at prioritization, heavy on task management, and product savvy. Given the high number of customers that they need to manage, CSMs in this segment need to be able to adapt quickly and be very efficient project managers. Being product knowledgeable and versed in the category your product belongs to is a huge plus. Customers want to know how to convert their needs into your product. They also want to know what other customers in the industry are doing, so it benefits everyone to be an industry watcher. Example profiles of persons with prior related experience and skills include Project and Program Managers, Support Reps (especially if your product is technically complex), and customer-facing Product Managers.

Small Business Customer Success Manager–to–Customer Ratio and CSM Profiles

In the Small Business segment, which has your smallest revenue customers, a CSM manages roughly $1–2M as the median, with 54% of Small Business Customer Success Managers managing less than $2M of ARR. A Small Business Customer Success Manager manages roughly 100–250 as the median, however 37% of CSMs in this segment manage more than 250 customers each (Figure 13.4). It's even more important in this segment to sharpen your digital outreaches and only focus your CSMs on customers with high risks to renewals or expansion or advocacy opportunities. By default, your team in this segment will be highly reactive.

In the Small Business segment, you typically want CSMs who are skilled at prioritization. If your product or service needs technical competence, most Small Business customers will not have the budget to spend on paid services from your company. They will expect the CSM to roll up their sleeves and work with their teams. In those cases, hiring people with excellent technical skills is advantageous. Example profiles of persons with prior experience and related skills include Solutions Architects, Sales Engineers, or Support Reps, especially if your product is technically complicated. If your product is simpler to set up, then Inside Sales Reps,

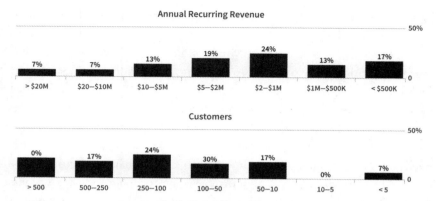

Figure 13.4   Small Business Customer Success Manager – ARR managed and customer ratios.

Business Development Managers or Account Managers can work well in this role.

Some companies implement a shared or a "pooled" Customer Success team. On this type of team, Small Business customers don't get a designated CSM. Instead, they get a pool of people, and the customer is managed by whoever has available capacity at any point in time. Patrick Eichen from Cornerstone OnDemand commented on this type of CS team. He stated: "When we scaled customer success for our mid-market and small business customers, we implemented a shared support model, meaning our clients don't have a dedicated resource. Instead, they work with a team of CSMs that support their market segment. When we made this change, it was important to us that our clients still felt that they could depend on us to help them achieve their desired outcomes, even if it meant they didn't have a person dedicated to them to help achieve this. Additionally, many of our smaller customers have limited resources and often can't invest a considerable amount of time to 'skill up' on our product. To ensure the success of our clients, we provide a variety of virtual engagement opportunities, all hosted by Customer Success Managers, so that clients can engage an expert and get the help they need."

Patrick further added, "In order to deliver on this model, we have invested heavily in our talent acquisition process. Aside from having various CS leaders vet out potential candidates we also conduct a situational based component within the interview process so that a candidate gets to go through an exercise that they will likely encounter in the field. This gives us a good line of sight into the specific skills we know a candidate needs to have to be successful – things like product knowledge, presentation skills, and the ability to overcome objections. It also allows the candidate a better perspective of a day in the life of a CSM within our organization. This approach has also provided us with greater internal talent mobility, giving our CSMs that were initially hired into a shared support role the opportunity to eventually develop and grow into a more dedicated role with larger customers."

Here's one final note, a cautionary one, related to determining your CSM ratios. Do your best to avoid using an arbitrary revenue per CSM target and working backwards (e.g. $2M per CSM). Doing so does not account for the desired outcomes you need to attain and could set you up for failure from the beginning. You should start your analysis by trying to determine the minimum amount of engagement that is required to attain your maximum retention and growth revenue targets. In other words, try to identify what activities and motions your CSMs must conduct that have the greatest impact on your company's performance objectives. Determine the level of effort required and the frequency of customer engagement across your various segments to help inform you of the number of CSMs you'll need to hit your revenue and growth targets. It's the same exercise any Sales Executive would go through in their planning efforts.

Compensating Your Customer Success Managers

There's no one-size-fits-all solution for compensation and structures for CSMs. It all depends on what you are trying to drive with that team at any point in time. This structure also implies that you'll need to evolve your design over time as you accomplish your goals for that measurement period (Figure 13.5).

The one principle that is widely adopted is to design the team's compensation in a way that depends on a fixed base while adding a variable portion on top. The most common model is 70–80% of the compensation tied to the fixed base and the remaining 20–30% tied to variable compensation. The variable compensation can be based on commissions,

Figure 13.5   Metrics to compensate your Customer Success Managers.

like a sales organization, if the primary role of the CSM is to manage renewals and upsell transactions. Many organizations use Account Managers for this task. Moving to more of a bonus-based compensation structure allows you to differentiate from the sales function and gives you the flexibility to evolve the metrics over time.

Next, it's important to decide what metrics drive the variable part of the compensation structure. If your CSM team is relatively new, and the maturity of the team is low, the primary objective should be to get consistent and predictable in their activities. At this stage, tying the variable compensation to completion of key events like Executive Business Reviews, onboarding processes, renewals milestones, or adoption review meetings with customers, helps ensure the team is developing the right Customer Success Management muscles. This stage is foundational, and the team must be doing the basic maneuvers before becoming more sophisticated in processes and metrics.

As the organization matures and activities become more predictable and consistent, you will find that many activities can get you to the same outcome. The Customer Success team, by this time, has developed the ability to recognize patterns and choose different playbooks based on the situation. However, it's not enough to just monitor those activities. You have to start measuring the impact of those activities which are the leading indicator outcomes. Examples would be improvements in product adoption metrics, improvement in Health Scores, improvement in the number of referenceable customers or an increase in expansion leads generated. These will tell you that your customers are heading to long-term success and hence revenue retention and growth for your business. At this stage, tying the variable compensation to the achievement of key leading indicator outcomes helps ensure that the team is evolving from activities to the impact that those activities are having with the customer base.

Finally, most of you likely work at for-profit companies. That means you need the CSM to make customers successful because successful customers drive retention and growth in your company's revenues. As the organization matures, you will need to track optimizing activities and leading indicators that drive towards the financial impact on your company. Financial outcomes are a lagging indicator, meaning that all of the actions have already taken place that can influence it. At this stage, tying the variable compensation to the achievement of key lagging financial outcomes, like gross retention rate, net retention rate, or upsell or cross-sell revenue, helps ensure that the team is evolving from leading indicators to the financial impact at your company. You might be tempted to start measuring and compensating your CSMs on the lagging financial outcomes to show the "value" of the team. Resist that temptation! You are doing the team and your company a disservice by building sophisticated processes and metrics before addressing the foundational processes.

If you are going through this maturity curve for the first time, here are some guiding timelines to help you think about the transition milestones:

- Start and stay in the activities stage for at least six months; this is the minimum time you'll need to get the team used to their processes and metrics.
- Stay in the leading indicators stage for at least 6 more months, preferably 12 months. Your team will get better at pattern recognition of the activities and leading outcomes.
- If your primary business challenge is avoiding churn, measure and compensate the team on gross retention rate or churn rate. Ideally, you can tie compensation to individual CSMs' portfolio of managed accounts or books of business. If they are not large enough or predictable enough, start with tying the compensation to the overall company retention or churn goals. If the primary business challenge is driving expansion in your customer base, compensate the CSMs on the upsells/cross-sells in their book of business.

Dashboards to Manage the Customer Success Team

As a leader of the CSM team, there are a few different types of dashboards you need to manage your team effectively; Table 13.1 provides a glimpse of your options.

Table 13.1   Dashboards to manage Customer Success teams.

Dashboards	Description	Purpose
Renewals Due by Quarter	Total ARR (Annual Recurring Revenue) up for renewal this quarter and subsequent quarters	Understand how much ARR is at stake this quarter and subsequent quarters
Churn/At-Risk this Quarter	Total ARR that has churned or is at-risk this quarter	Understand the "worst-case scenario" for ARR this quarter
Customers Across Stages	Number of customers by stage	See where your customers are in the customer journey
Average NPS Score	Average of NPS (Net Promoter Score) across all customers	Evaluate the Customer Experience scores across customers
Accounts and ARR by Customer Success Manager	Total accounts and ARR across various Customer Success Managers	Identify who has more capacity and who doesn't

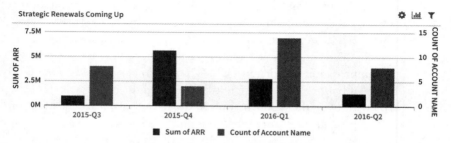

Figure 13.6   Renewals due by quarter.

Renewals Due by Quarter

This report (Figure 13.6) helps leaders of CSM teams understand the total renewal revenue at stake by quarter. It's essential to understand both the count of customers as well as the dollar value of those renewals. In one case, you may have a high number of customers up for renewal in the current quarter, but the total dollar amount may be relatively small. The team leader will likely be less involved with each of the renewals because of the total number of customers. On the other hand, you may have a quarter with a relatively small number of customers representing a high dollar renewal amount. In this latter case, team leaders will have the visibility in advance to be more intimately involved with each of these high-value renewal customers.

Churn/At-Risk this Quarter and High-Risk Customers

Extending the renewals report further, you can understand which of the renewals in the current quarter are at risk based on the Health Scores of those customers. Assuming you have an accurate model, the customer Health Score should ultimately be an indicator of renewability. When you combine renewal information and customer health into one view (Figure 13.7), you can more easily assess how many renewal dollars are at potential risk in current and forthcoming quarters (Figure 13.8) and take appropriate action in advance with the associated customers.

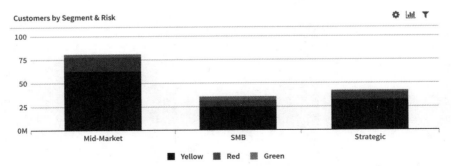

Figure 13.7   Renewals by segment and Health Score (risk).

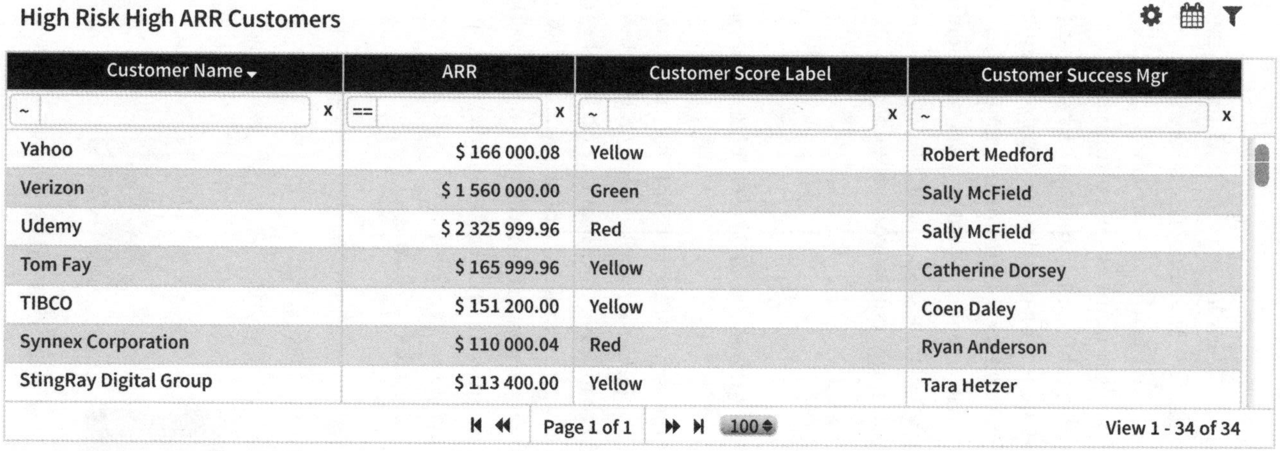

High Risk High High ARR Customers

Customer Name ▾	ARR	Customer Score Label	Customer Success Mgr
Yahoo	$ 166 000.08	Yellow	Robert Medford
Verizon	$ 1 560 000.00	Green	Sally McField
Udemy	$ 2 325 999.96	Red	Sally McField
Tom Fay	$ 165 999.96	Yellow	Catherine Dorsey
TIBCO	$ 151 200.00	Yellow	Coen Daley
Synnex Corporation	$ 110 000.04	Red	Ryan Anderson
StingRay Digital Group	$ 113 400.00	Yellow	Tara Hetzer

◄◄ ◄ Page 1 of 1 ►► ► 100 ◆   View 1 - 34 of 34

Figure 13.8 High-risk high-revenue customers.

Customers Across Lifecycle Stages

This report (Figure 13.9) helps leaders understand the distribution of customers across various lifecycle stages. You will be able to see the impact of work on specific teams vs. others. If customers are stuck in a particular stage for a long time, that also causes concern.

Average NPS Score

This report (Figure 13.10) gives a quick view of trends in Net Promoter Scores over time to see if customers' perceptions of Customer Experience are improving or deteriorating over time.

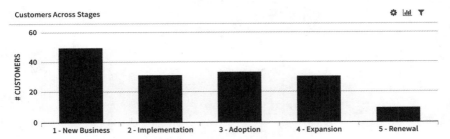

Figure 13.9   Customers across Lifecycle stages.

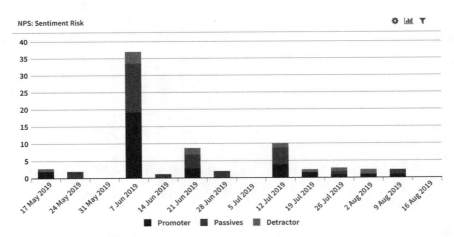

Figure 13.10   Net Promoter Scores over time.

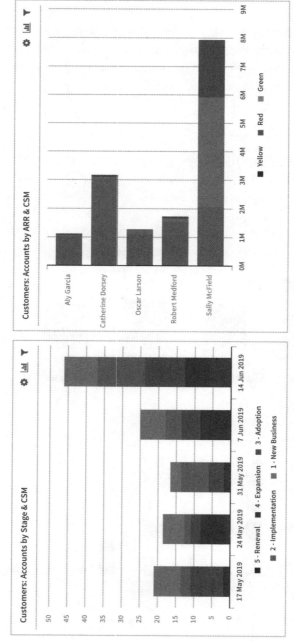

Figure 13.11 Accounts managed per CSM.

Accounts and ARR by Customer Success Manager

This report (Figure 13.11) identifies if certain CSMs are more "loaded" than others. It will help you decide future capacity planning. It also helps to know if certain CSMs have more customers in a particular lifecycle stage or Health Score implying increased workloads at any point in time.

● ● ●

As a leader of a Customer Success team, this chapter has aimed to give you some tools to think about how to best organize your team according to customer needs and the skills available on your team. It also showed you the possibilities to incentivize your CSMs to follow the right behaviors and how to create dashboards and charts to manage the team. Don't be afraid to customize these tools to fit your organization best. As you move forward, you will find ways to help you design the optimal career paths for CSMs and frameworks to measure career progression.

14

Creating Career Paths for Your Customer Success Managers

In the previous chapter, we discussed the need for multiple "types" of Customer Success Managers. Depending on the needs of each customer segment, these teammates have different skills and aspirations for their roles. We believe that this topic not only deserves its own chapter, it also deserves its own separate author. For this task, we asked Nadav Shem-Tov, Director of Teammate Success-Customer Success at Gainsight. Since joining the Gainsight family, he has moved strategically into roles within our organization that benefited from his knowledge of Customer Success and his ability to create a career path infrastructure for our CSMs. He was also a CSM and Director of Customer Success. Who better to give you a glimpse into CS career pathing than the individual who does it for us.

Designing CSM as a Career

By Nadav Shem-Tov

When we were building out and scaling the Customer Success organization at Gainsight, we encountered several challenges surrounding the issue of career paths. As our CSMs gained experience in their roles, they wanted to see a trajectory that reflected their abilities and their desire to do new things. Some of them wanted to continue being an individual contributor CSM. Others had aspirations of managing people. Some even had their eyes on the C-Suite. No matter the goal of the individual, each member of the Customer Success team wanted more clarity on their role requirements and expectations. They also wanted to know how their roles might change with future growth. We found that having a career path for the Customer Success team was imperative. We share our approach, which is a collage of many best practices in Human Resources (also called People Teams) adjusted to our own needs, in the hope it will help you acquire and retain top talent in an industry that is growing rapidly and evolving at breakneck speeds.

Career pathing involves developing a consistent framework for organizing the different jobs or roles within your Customer Success team. It begins with dividing all of them into distinct levels that are tied to specific skills, expectations, titles, and compensation structures. Producing such a framework promotes meaningful career conversations with your team members and ensures that your CSMs have clear paths to continue to grow and develop their careers. If the framework is consistent and objective, it will advance your efforts to ensure that teammates feel like they have visibility into their own careers and what it takes to get them to the next level. This same framework could also contribute to an environment of diversity and inclusion with more consistency and pay parity.

Creating Career Paths within the CS Function

Creating a comprehensive framework for career pathing might seem like a daunting task, but in our experience, developing a simple framework early and then evolving it over time is the right approach. The good news is that some companies now have a member of the People Team designated to work with the CS team – often called a People Business Partner. Work closely with your People leadership to ensure they understand the nuances of this rapidly evolving profession. We'll share our blueprint for creating career paths with you here.

Step 1: Define the Different CS Jobs in Your Organization

The first step is to define the different jobs that exist in your CS organization. Typically, there are at least two types in a Customer Success organization: An Individual Contributor (IC) Customer Success Manager, and a Manager or Leader of CSMs.

In larger organizations, there might be additional CSM role types that have unique definitions. An example is a Customer Success Architect. This job is more technical in nature than a traditional CSM. Another is a Customer Success Operations Manager that is more focused on strategy, operations, and enablement versus direct client management.

There are also distinctions between different Customer Success Manager jobs based on segments; such as an SMB Customer Success Manager versus an Enterprise Customer Success Manager. Whether these should be thought of as completely separate *jobs* or as different *levels* within the same role depends on the uniqueness of each job description. More specifically, the skills required to do each of these jobs. For instance, SMB Customer Success Managers and Enterprise Customer Success Managers require similar skills, but you need your Enterprise Customer Success Managers to have a more advanced level of mastery of these skills. We'll explain further as we proceed through the chapter.

Step 2: Create Distinct Levels for Each Job

Once you have your distinct CSM jobs defined, it's time to determine their different levels. A job-level describes the impact, expectations, and seniority required for a specific role. Many commonly used career-level frameworks designate six levels for an individual contributor job like a CSM. For management or leadership jobs, like a Director or Manager of CSMs, a higher number of levels are used, often eight. This number should allow for the full span of manager levels in your CS organization; starting from an emerging CS Team Lead up to your Chief Customer Officer.

Let's assume you defined just two different jobs for your CS organization: Customer Success Manager (IC) and a Manager of CSMs. There is a need to develop clear, distinct levels for each of these jobs or "tracks" that ideally include specific responsibilities, scope, titles, experiences, and skill requirements. These distinctions will create a clear transparent map of potential roles for individuals on your team. (See Tables 14.1 and 14.2.)

In the example above, it is essential to develop two separate career tracks (Individual Contributor vs. Manager). Doing so opens up a career growth trajectory for individuals who want to specialize in the actual Customer Success Manager job from a technical/customer skills point of view, and other individuals who seek people management positions.

You should strive to ensure that different levels for each of your Customer Success jobs are tied to salary and total compensation bands based on current market data, which can differ by geographic location. If an existing framework exists based on a standard methodology, ensure your level definitions align with the general market definitions. This is critical in ensuring you use the correct data for benchmarking things like compensation. Be forewarned, however, that even popular salary benchmark reports are immature in assessing the new Customer Success Profession. They may not appropriately map CS titles, so work with your People Teams to align on the right compensation ranges.

One thing to consider is, depending on your talent strategy and model for your CS organization, you may not need all these different levels in your organization. The number of actual CSM positions on your team for each of the levels will depend on your organizational design, product complexity, industry maturity, business model, and budget, among other factors.

Step 3: Define Critical Skills Needed for Each Job

Once you have your jobs and levels defined, it is important to get clarity on the required critical skills. These are the skills that will drive successful outcomes for each of the CSM jobs. The baseline skills should be the same for each job, but they will have increasing expectations or requirements as you move up the levels. See Table 14.2. The skills should include a mix of the three core CS competencies described in Chapter 4: knowledge mastery, problem-solving, and building relationships with your customer. We recommend starting by defining five critical skills per CSM job. The suggested number is a good trade-off between being comprehensive and

Table 14.1 Customer Success Manager – individual contributor job levels.

	CSM 1	CSM 2	CSM 3	CSM 4	CSM 5	CSM 6
Title	Customer Success Associate	Senior Customer Success Associate	Customer Success Manager	Senior Customer Success Manager	Customer Success Director	Senior Customer Success Director
Scope	Assists Customer Success Managers in administrative tasks	Assists Customer Success Managers and starts managing clients on their own	Manages own book of business	Manages a more strategic book of business/more complex clients	Manages a strategic book of business and serves as a mentor/coach to other team members	Manages most complex clients and serves as a thought-leader in the industry
Typical profile	Recent grad with no job experience	Early career employee	Experienced Customer Success Manager professional	Seasoned/ Senior professional	Very Advanced/ Seasoned professional	A true expert

Table 14.2 Customer Success Manager – people manager job levels.

	Mgr 1	Mgr 2	Mgr 3	Mgr 4	Mgr 5	Mgr 6	Mgr 7
Title	Team Lead, Customer Success	Senior Team Lead, Customer Success	Manager, Customer Success	Senior Manager, Customer Success	Director, Customer Success	Senior Director, Customer Success	VP, Customer Success
Scope	Manages a small number of more junior individuals, might be hybrid role as IC	Manages a number of individuals, might still be hybrid role as IC	Manages a full team of Customer Success Managers	Manages a larger/more strategic team of Customer Success Managers	Manages multiple Customer Success Manager teams, Manager of Managers; responsibility for planning/strategic priorities	Manages multiple Customer Success Manager teams, likely more strategic/complex Manager of Managers; fully responsible for planning/strategic priorities	Oversees the entire CS organization across all segments and jobs
Typical profile	New to people management	Junior Manager, might be hybrid role as IC	Experienced Manager	Likely has been a successful Manager for some time	A senior manager with strategic/executive's skills	Has proven him/herself as a Director	Executive-level individual

flexible, while still being a digestible number of skills to discuss and track with your team.

When developing the list of skills required for a specific job, you should balance between being overly specific and being too general. There is an obvious need for a comprehensive collection of skills that covers the core requirements of the job. However, you must also emphasize specific behaviors and nuances that you know would make CSMs successful on your team.

Here are some example critical skills for a Strategic or Enterprise Customer Success Manager:

- **Domain expertise:** achieves expert status on industry best practices and applies them to client situations by leveraging our standard methodology.
- **Product and use-case expertise:** achieves expert status on supported products and is able to identify how they can solve key use-cases and challenges for customers.
- **Problem-solving:** proactively manages and owns the work process to drive desired outcomes; uses a hypothesis-driven approach to cover and solve key client problems, and prioritizes work by focusing on what's most important.
- **Prescriptive approach:** uses a prescriptive approach to drive client decisions and align key stakeholders towards action, including challenging clients to change course when needed
- **Cross-functional collaboration:** effectively collaborates with other teammates and teams to drive client outcomes and company outcomes.

If your CSMs need to be more technical in their roles or manage a higher customer ratio per CSM, here are some examples of critical skills. Note that most remain the same with nuances for product and technical skills:

- **Domain expertise:** achieves expert status on industry best practices and applies them to client situations by leveraging our standard methodology.
- **Product and use-case expertise:** achieves expert status on supported products and is able to identify how they can solve key use-cases and challenges for customers.
- **Technical skills:** configuring your product/service to enable client outcomes

- **Problem-solving:** uses a hypothesis-driven approach to cover and solve key client problems, and prioritizes work by focusing on what's most important (80/20).
- **Prescriptive approach:** uses a prescriptive approach to drive client decisions and align key stakeholders towards action, including challenging clients to change course when needed.
- **Cross-functional collaboration:** effectively collaborates with other teams to drive client outcomes and company outcomes.

Step 4: Map the Critical Skills to Each Job and Level

Now that your CS-related job skills are clearly defined, the next step is to apply them to the specific levels within each job. Be sure to build increasing expectations for the demonstrated level of mastery for each skill as you move up the individual levels. Table 14.3 provides an example of a three-level CSM job framework and the associated skills expectations.

Laying out the skills in clear terms and providing the appropriate visibility to your CS team will help drive meaningful conversations such as, "Which career track am I better suited to or more interested in, Individual Contributor vs. Management track?", "What are the required skills I should develop to attain the next level in my career as a Customer Success Professional?", and "How can I develop these skills?"

Step 5: Roll it Out to Your Team

Now for our last and final step: rolling out this methodology and applying it consistently across the employee lifecycle. This might sound simple, but as every good Customer Success Manager and Manager of CSMs knows, roll out and change management is an iterative and demanding process.

Here are a few things to consider when introducing a new career pathing framework to your CS team:

- Ensure that all managers in your team are intimately familiar with the details and nuances of the framework you've developed. If managers are well informed, the Customer Success team will trust that this process works for them.

Table 14.3 Example mapping of a core skill to job levels.

	CSM 3	CSM 4	CSM 5
Critical Skill #5: Pre-scriptive Approach	■ Mostly understands key client stakeholders and their influence and decision-making powers ■ Focuses client interactions on driving actions and follow-through ■ Provides prescriptive guidance to clients even when it differs from their current point of view or approach (challenger mentality); might still require some supervisor backup and guidance at times	■ Strong ability to identify key client stakeholders and their influence and decision-making powers, including in situations where they're ambiguous ■ Focuses client interactions on driving actions and follow-through, and able to influence clients and hold them accountable for follow-up actions ■ Provides strong prescriptive guidance to clients even when it differs from their current point of view or approach (challenger mentality); knows when and how to leverage other external contacts	■ Expert in identifying key client stakeholders and their influence and decision-making powers – able to assess and analyze them quickly and effectively, and get to the bottom of the influence map even in the most complex and ambiguous situations ■ Focuses client interactions on driving actions and follow-through, and able to influence clients and hold them accountable for follow-up actions ■ Provides strong prescriptive guidance to clients even when it differs from their current point of view or approach (challenger mentality), even in the most sensitive and challenging situations ■ Able to mentor and guide other teammates in challenging client situations

- It is important to remember that while career pathing provides a good roadmap for potential tracks and career growth for your Customer Success Managers, your ability to promote an individual will depend on multiple factors, such as the specific individual's mastery of the required skills for the job and level. The other aspect is the availability and actual organizational need for that specific job and level within your team, as dictated by your talent strategy, budget, and workforce planning practices. Just because someone has the skills required to become a manager does not automatically mean your team needs another manager. Consider the individual achieving the expected skill mastery for the next level as a necessity. However, there must be a matching business need to establish a condition for promotion.
- Your planning and talent strategy should ideally allow you to create rough timelines for career paths and moving up the levels of an individual job. For example, 12–24 months to move from CSM 3 to CSM 4. The specifics will depend on your unique company situation of course.

Conducting a Comprehensive Talent Review Process

In the context of career pathing, promotions, and performance, we recommend that you periodically conduct a talent review process to methodically assess your current talent pool and align on action plans. Many companies have a company-wide process. Even if your company doesn't, it is something you can definitely launch within your CS team.

A common framework that is still being used for talent reviews is the 9-Block Talent Model developed in the 1970s by McKinsey and General Electric (GE) (Figure 14.1). It now has many versions and interpretations. At its core, it helps you map all of the individuals in your team across two main axes: their *current* performance in their role, and their *future/potential* level of contribution to your organization. These axes might be called many different names, but we like thinking about them as Performance and Promotability, respectively.

While the 9-Block Talent Model can be particularly helpful when used consistently throughout your company for a variety of strategic people initiatives, you could use a version of it within your team to drive promotion, performance, and development decisions.

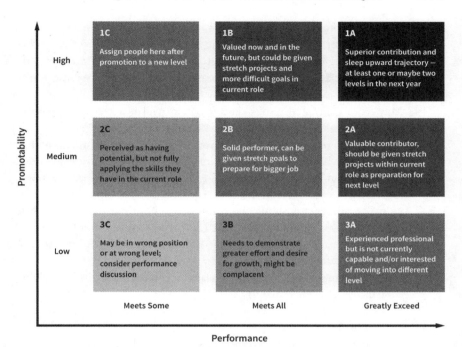

Figure 14.1   Example 9-block grid for talent assessment.

To launch a talent review process within your team, we recommend you follow these steps:

1. **Align** on the exact framework to use in your organization. Specifically, determine what factors you will use for your process and what are the related assessment criteria. The more specific you can be with defining your criteria, the more likely you are to minimize unconscious and irrelevant biases that might cloud your assessment. For Performance specifically, you should utilize your work from Step 4 above and use the specific skill expectations for an individual's level as the measure for Performance.

2. **Assess** each of the individuals on your team across the two factors. This would mean that you or the direct manager of these individuals should assign a rating for Performance. For example: Meets Some, Meets All, Exceeds; and a rating for Promotability, such as Low, Medium, High.

3. **Calibrate** these assessments across your leadership team. This is an important step to ensure assessments are in line with the view of other leaders in the organizations. This step, if done correctly, can also help minimize or at least expose common biases that might get in the way of the initial assessment.

4. **Map** your calibrated results on a 9-block grid to get a single view of your entire talent pool. See Figure 14.1.

5. **Act** on the results of the talent review. Placement of an individual in a specific block should indicate what specific actions are in order. Placement on the block should also be used to help determine when individuals are ready for promotion. For example (see Figure 14.1), individuals in Block 1A should be promoted within the next year, while those in Block 2B are typically at least a year away from promotion. This entire exercise will prove futile unless you and your team use it to develop specific action plans:

   - Development or promotion plans for individuals in the right-hand-side of the 9-block.
   - Performance and development plans for individuals in the left-hand-side.

6. **Repeat regularly.** We recommend you follow the full process twice a year, with a more minor refresh quarterly.

Creating Career Paths Between Functions

Creating a career path for your Customer Success Managers within the CS function as described above is definitely where you should start. But some of the most advanced companies treat their Customer Success talent pool even more strategically, both as a *consumer* for talent from other functions, and a *supplier* of top talent for other organizations in the company.

As a CS leader, you are surely aware of the agonizing ramp-up period for new CSMs who join your company – the time it takes a new CSM to learn everything they need about your company, how you "do things" at your company, your product, and your CS operational processes. More often than not, this period seems longer than it should be, especially when you have unassigned customers who can't wait for their new CSM to be assigned. What if there was a way to shorten this ramp-up period?

Relying on internal talent might just be the answer. This might sound like common sense, but CS leaders so often turn externally when recruiting for new CSMs and forget to look internally. Encouraging internal mobility from other departments into the CS team can be a successful strategy as it will likely cut down the time new Customer Success Managers spend learning how the company operates and what its products are all about.

A good place to start is comparing the necessary skills you defined for the different CS jobs (at the beginning of this chapter) and identifying other roles in your company that require or help develop some of the same skills. For Customer Success Manager jobs, we recommend looking at roles such as a Sales Development Representative (SDR), Support Agents, Account Managers or Renewal Representatives, Solution Consultants, Project Managers, and Business Analysts.

Once you have identified some roles that could serve as a good talent pool for your CS jobs, work together with leaders of these groups and your People team to develop a program to encourage transitions and mobility into CS roles. Here are some things you may consider as you build a similar program:

- **Milestones.** What are the specific milestones or points in time in which individuals would be considered for a CSM position? For example, after 18 months as an SDR, you can apply for a CSM role.
- **Process and decision criteria.** What is the process for interviewing and evaluating internal candidates once they've hit their milestones? What are the decision criteria that will be used to evaluate them and what will the transition look like?
- **Skills development.** A good program should also provide mechanisms to bridge any skills gaps that might exist through formal and informal Learning and Development opportunities for interested individuals. For example, an SDR might have 3 out of the 5 critical skills needed to be a Customer Success Manager. These programs could include formal supplementary courses or more informal mentoring and shadowing programs.
- **Positioning.** How will you build awareness of the CS career path within other departments across your company? How will you market the CS profession as a solid career choice for individuals currently in other jobs?

Conclusion

Our journey together is winding down but is certainly not over. We have only scratched the surface of what is a growing compendium of Customer Success best practices, various tactics, practical tips, and management and operational frameworks that are being developed and refined every day across the globe. You've heard from many amazing voices and seasoned leaders about their insights and real lessons from the field.

We've learned that Customer Success was borne out of a critical gap created as a result of software moving to the cloud and the advent of the subscription economy. No one function was responsible for making sure that the customer was attaining their desired expectations. More importantly, no one was ultimately responsible for ensuring the customer would stay a customer and buy more from you. Customers wanted an assured outcome delivered with a great experience.

The CSM role was thrust into the middle of this business revolution and became the qualified individual chartered to drive value for the customer. The new profession encompassed a new collection of competencies and expertise that had previously been distributed across many different job functions. Interestingly, little did anyone anticipate that this new CSM role, because of its influential scope of responsibilities and high level of customer intimacy, would be one of the best catalysts for rapid career advancement – truly #successforall.

Customer Success is a remarkable and rewarding profession. There is a real joy you experience when you help people succeed and businesses grow. If you have great ambition, love engaging with people, and like solving complex problems, Customer Success Management may very well be the best place for you. But, be ready for challenges! Being a Customer Success Manager is not easy. It's a job that requires relentless effort to deliver outcomes and exceptional experiences to every customer you engage. If you are new to Customer Success, we hope this book gave you the direction and some initial steps to becoming an outstanding Customer Success Manager.

As a manager and leader of Customer Success teams, you too have a very challenging job of making sure you are providing your CS team with the right direction, removing obstacles for them in their daily work and being a partner in driving their long-term careers. We wholeheartedly hope that the frameworks, example processes, and job descriptions in the book make your job a little easier to better attract and retain awesome talent.

Lastly, at its core, Customer Success is a human endeavor. We are not alone on this journey. As you make rapid progress in your respective careers, we implore you to give back to the Customer Success community. Share what you've learned. Find someone new to CS. Tell your success stories and impart your enthusiasm about them. Join local and virtual CS community groups. Share your challenges and new ideas. Write blogs and broadcast your learnings for the betterment of your peers. Together, we can raise the bar for everyone that benefits from the positive impact of a more effective community of Customer Success professionals. We wish you all the best of success!

Acknowledgments

From Ashvin

When I first heard about the opportunity to write this book, I knew it would be a challenging yet rewarding job. Ruben and I realized we had the responsibility and incredible opportunity to channel the years of our work, as well as the influence of our entire Customer Success community, into writing. I owe a tremendous amount of gratitude to our Customer Success colleagues who pour out endless hours of energy every day, every week, and every month to make their customers successful. They make mistakes, learn from them, and share their learnings with the CS community to improve the outcomes for their customers and Customer Success professionals worldwide. Thank you all for allowing us the opportunity to share all our learnings through this book.

I am fortunate in my career to have had wonderful mentors who have inspired me to push myself more than I could have on my own. I'm eternally grateful to Kamal Haddad, Ray Casey, James Dillon, and Badri Kothandaraman for recruiting me at Cypress Semiconductor – my first job in Silicon Valley. They encouraged me to try new roles and got me hooked on the amazing world of working with customers and solving tough problems. I must acknowledge that one of my best educational experiences was at McKinsey & Company. I owe so much to the firm for giving me the courage to believe that no problem is unsolvable. The education I received from Marc Singer, Dan Leberman, Alexis Krivkovich, Brian Gregg, Roxane Divol, Monica Adractas, Robert Byrne, Barry Ames, Abid Mohsin, Alfonso

245

Pulido and Kausik Rajgopal about executive communications and creative problem-solving are priceless. Most importantly, thanks to all of them for letting me make mistakes and learn from them.

I come now to the crowning glory of my working career – Gainsight. There are so many people to thank. Thank you to Nick Mehta and Allison Pickens for believing in me and letting me join you at the forefront of a new and thriving category. Nick Mehta, you've been the most inspirational CEO and human being I've ever worked with. You've taught me how to win at business while being human first and the importance of leading by example. Thank you, Allison Pickens, for taking innumerable chances with me. You've given me the space to create things from scratch, watched my back when I made mistakes, and you have always been available to trade notes and ideas. Thanks to my amazing former and current teammates Nadav Shem-Tov, Ganesh Subramanian, Tyler McNally, Kellie Capote, Kelly DeHart, Barr Moses, Easton Taylor, Emily McDaniel, Peter Wride, Daniel Levine, Tony Smart, Sridhar Gollapalli, Elaine Cleary, Seth Wylie, Rich Busch, Davi Shorter, and many others for making our customers, investors, and teammates successful. A special thanks to Allison Pickens, Priyanka Srinivasan, and Seth Wylie for all the work on Gainsight Elements. It had a significant impact on this book.

This book would not be possible without the editorial team at Wiley, in particular, Richard Narramore, Vicki Adang, and Victoria Anllo. My first foray into writing a book would not have happened without your impressive guidance along the way. A huge shout-out to our Developmental Editor, Martta Eicher Rabago. You took my scribbles, thoughts, and mumblings, and gave them a voice. You were patient and encouraging when the process looked impossible. You made sure I brought my best to every word and chapter in this book. Thank you Martta!

A very special thank you to Brian Millham for generously providing the foreword of this book. Your founding efforts at Salesforce has been pivotal to the customer success profession.

I saved the most important dedication for last. To my wife Ragini and my daughter Shaira, you make me a better human being every day. You were selfless in giving me the space to create this book. I'm sorry for all the weekends when I was absent in your lives busy writing. I can safely say that the book would not have happened without your endless support and love through this process. I'm so lucky to have you both in my life. To my mom and dad, thank you for making me who I am. You have sacrificed a lot in your own lives to make sure I got to where I am today. Please know that I'm thankful each and every day to have the best parents in the whole wide world.

I hope this book takes our Customer Success Community one step further in our evolution. If you find the book valuable, please share it with your friends and colleagues. Happy Success for All!

From Ruben

When I learned that Ashvin and I were going on a book-writing adventure together, I knew right away that there was a missing variable to its successful completion. Every good book that withstands all types of weather has a strong binding. The binding serves as the book's spine so that it can stand upright and on its own. It is the glue that keeps all the pages tightly structured, presenting it as a singular, consistent form. The binding must also be remarkably malleable, flexing but not breaking, as each chapter turns and a new one begins. Throughout this entire project, and for the nearly 30 years we've been together, my binding has been my wife, Martta. She encouraged me when I was in doubt. She extorted words when I thought there were none left to share. She poured herself selflessly into my work. She took on everything in our home life that I couldn't do while pulling 80–90-hour weeks. This project, and my career, for that matter, would not have happened without her. In fact, if you look at the Copyright page of this book, you will find her credited as the Developmental Editor, which is factually one of her many talents and functionally her material role in this project. Thank you, my love.

To all my children: your sacrifice and support have always been my inspiration. Don't ever give up on your aspirations and embrace the unpredictability of life. To my mom and dad: thank you for your unconditional love, providing me with a solid foundation and an abundance of privileges that led me here. I am forever grateful. To my brother, thank you for your generous heart and your always sincere desire for me and our family's happiness. To my now departed mother- and father-in-law, your steadiness, wisdom, and good counsel are reflected in this work. Thank you for teaching me the true meaning of The Word. To my extended family and friends, thank you always for your shared enthusiasm. A distinct thank you to Joan Johnson for the use of your beautiful SoCal home as a two-week writing retreat. It served as a sanctuary on so many levels. May you be forever blessed. To my number one mentor, Yitzhak Ben-Zvi, thank you for always believing in me and imparting the truth that every situation can result in a win–win.

Thank you, Anthony Kennada, for your genuine friendship and fateful advocacy (and book cover idea). You have truly impacted my life forever. Thank you, Dan Steinman, for your mentorship, bringing me on board, and the many conversations we had from across the pond. Thank you, Nick Mehta, for being living proof of #humanfirst leadership, always being your authentic self, and embracing me as part of the Gainsight family, starting even from the day you interviewed me. Thank you Ashvin Vaidyanathan, for the opportunity to partner with you on this quest. I truly appreciate you. Of course, none of this would have been possible without Jim Eberlin and Sreedhar Peddineni, Gainsight's founders.

This book is a reflection of all Gainsters past and present – I just happened to be one the scribes. To my original CS cohort, Elaine, Kelly D., Tracy, Julia, Paul P., and Nikka, this book is your work too. Special thanks to all my Phoenix teammates, especially the other crazy guy who decided to join me as PHX #2, Mike Manheimer, as we worked out of a temporary North Scottsdale office/storage closet loaned to us by Scott Salkin back in the day. So many good memories, such as moving downtown (three times) and naming our new conference rooms after Mexican-style meats because we were hungry that day. I appreciate you, Mike, and Lauren Sommers for your encouragement, giving me latitude on deadlines and limiting new assignments for the three months while keeping me contained to no more than two full-time jobs. Thanks to Mervin John for helping me launch Pulse+ and for keeping the lights on during this book project. A big shout out to Ryan Anderson for curating all 50+ images and figures we needed for this text and for doing it on an outlandish timeline. Thanks to Priyanka Srinivasan, Seth Wylie, Allison Pickens, and Ashvin for the CS-Elements content peppered throughout this book. A literary thank you to Matthew Klassen, our principal wordsmithing craftsman and Head of Creative.

Your kind spirit and facetiousness are keenly reflected in Gainsight's written voice; much of it echoed herein.

A huge thank you to the amazing team at Wiley, in particular, Richard Narramore, Vicki Adang, Beula Jaculin and Victoria Anllo, for your amazing guidance and encouragement throughout this entire process. It was very meta to be on the receiving end of your "customer success" best practices playbook for first-time authors.

A very special thank you to Brian Millham for honoring us with the foreword of this book. Your pioneering work at Salesforce is one of the reasons customer success exists in the first place.

Finally, thank you to ALL of the incredible thought leaders that contributed to the project as well as the entire Customer Success Community. Thank you for the opportunity to share our voice. I hope this work serves to edify you. Cheers and success for all!

About the Authors

Ashvin Vaidyanathan is the Chief Customer Officer at Gainsight – the Customer Success Company. In his role, Ashvin manages the Customer Success, Professional Services, Education, and Technical Support teams. Ashvin started at Gainsight as a Customer Success Manager and spent a lot of his early years at Gainsight building new and innovative processes for CSMs. Prior to Gainsight, Ashvin was at McKinsey & Company consulting with companies on Marketing, Sales and Customer Experience transformations. When not at Gainsight, Ashvin is an advisor at Not In Our Town – a not for profit organization that uses documentary film and new media to stop hate and address bullying. He lives in San Francisco with his beautiful wife and daughter.

    Ruben Rabago, Gainsight's Chief Strategist, brings subject matter expertise to Pulse global CS programs, including worldwide conferences, CxO Summits, regional CS meetups, and various speaking engagements. He launched Pulse+, a refreshed continuation of the world's largest education and certification program for Customer Success professionals and provides curriculum guidance to universities. Ruben also leads Gainsight's community outreach intended to elevate diversity in the CS profession, including women returning to the workforce, military veterans, and other underrepresented persons. He was one of Gainsight's first CSMs and has more than 20 years of experience establishing and leading Customer and Product teams in traditional and SaaS-based companies including Scinet, WebMD, Sage Software, Carefx, Harris Corp, and WebPT, which includes three successful start-ups to acquisition. Ruben serves as mentor and advisor to CS leaders and professionals around the globe, consults and delivers custom training in support of digital transformation initiatives to businesses, from start-ups to Fortune 500. He's is a proud graduate of the University of Arizona, a free-time musician, and currently resides in North Phoenix with his wife and children.

Index

Page references followed by f and t indicate an illustrated figures and tables.